Dedication

For my devoted and determined husband David, who always believes in me and loves me in every muumuu.

Contents

Middle-Aged Mama in a Muumuu

The Marketing Magic Behind My 150x Growth –
A No-BS Playbook for Every Practitioner, Healer, &
Coach Who's Been Told "Nope, Not You"

Dr. Brandy Zachary, DC, IFMCP, FMACP

Also by author:

How to Read a Client From Across the Room (McGraw-Hill, NY)

**A Practitioner's Guide to Mastering Functional Medicine Lab Values –
Foundations of Health Testing** (Part 1 of 4)
Base-Level Blood Labs, Cardiometabolic, & Nutrition

**A Practitioner's Guide to Mastering Functional Medicine Lab Values – Gut &
Digestion** (Part 2 of 4)
Advanced Testing for Gastrointestinal Health

**A Practitioner's Guide to Mastering Functional Medicine Lab Values –
Hormonal Health & Balance** (Part 3 of 4)
Panels for Reproductive, Adrenal, and Thyroid Function

**A Practitioner's Guide to Mastering Functional Medicine Lab Values –
Metabolic Health & Toxin Testing** (Part 4 of 4)
Autoimmunity, Toxins, and Advanced Metabolic Markers

The **Dr.Z**® | Functional Medicine Academy

The Dr. Z Functional Medicine Academy, LLC
Sheridan, WY 82801

Copyright

Book Cover by eBookLaunch
Book formatting by David Zachary & Angel Tandoc
1st Edition 2025

Library of Congress Control Number - LCCN: 2025902709
ISBN 979-8-9927347-0-6 paperback
ISBN 979-8-9927347-1-2 hardcover
ISBN 979-8-9927347-2-0 ebook

Warning - Disclaimer
Dr. Brandy Zachary, DC, IFMCP, FMACP and The Dr. Z Functional Medicine Academy, have designed this book to provide information in regards to the subject matter covered. It is sold with the understanding that the publisher and the author is not liable for the misconception or misuse of information provided. The purpose of this book is to educate. It is not intended as a substitute for marketing or business training, or professional advice such as legal or financial counsel. Information in this book should not be construed as a promise of any outcome for any person or business. Make sure you always operate within your scope of practice, marketing and business best practices applicable to all local, state, and federal regulatory laws.

Publisher's Cataloging-in-Publication Data
Names: Zachary, Brandy, author.
Title: Middle-aged mama in a muumuu : the marketing magic behind my 150x growth – a no-bs playbook for every practitioner, healer, & coach who's been told "Nope, not you" / Dr. Brandy Zachary, DC, IFMCP, FMACP,
Description: Sales Wit & Humor | Sheridan, WY: The Dr. Z Functional Medicine LabDX, LLC, 2025.
Identifiers: LCCN: 2025902709 | ISBN: 979-8-9927347-1-2 (hardcover) | 979-8-9927347-0-6 (paperback) | 979-8-9927347-2-0 (ebook)
Subjects: LCSH Medical care—Marketing. | Branding (Marketing) | Marketing. | Success in business. | BISAC BUSINESS & ECONOMICS / Industries / Healthcare | BUSINESS & ECONOMICS / Marketing / General
Classification: LCC RA410.56 .Z33 2025 | DDC 362.1/068/8—dc23

For information about special pricing for bulk purchases, sales promotions, fundraising, and educational needs contact The Dr. Z Functional Medicine Academy, LLC at Team@TheDrZ.com or 1-307-291-9885 or visit the author's website at **www.TheDrZ.com**
Printed in the United States of America.
The Dr. Z is a registered trademark of Dr. Brandy Zachary, DC, IFMCP, FMACP.
Published by The Dr. Z Functional Medicine Academy, LLC 30 N Gould St Ste R #37288, Sheridan, WY 37288

Preface

Not Supposed to Happen...But It Did

At 49, I did something completely irrational—or perhaps, entirely brave. I packed up my life, turned 50 in a new country and decided that this was the moment to finally go all in on building the business I had always wanted.

Menopause had hit like a wrecking ball. I was the heaviest I'd ever been, my hormones were laughing at me from some cruel, invisible dimension, and the humidity had my hair in a permanent state of rebellion. The only outfit that made sense? A **muumuu**—with biker shorts underneath—because if my thighs rubbed together any harder, I was pretty sure I'd start a fire.

This was **not** the picture of a polished, power-playing entrepreneur. But, heck, when has reality ever looked like those Instagram-perfect success stories?

I had no fancy office. No professional video setup. No slick branding. Just me, a Zoom call, a ukulele, my dog, and a first attempt at running an ad that—if we're being honest—was completely lame.

And yet, to everyone's shock (including mine), that goofy, thrown-together ad damn near hit six figures in its first month. The momentum took off like wildfire.

Before I knew it, I had scaled so fast I was able to buy my way into the eight-figure boardroom—*barely* qualifying, mind you. And let me tell you, that room was *not* designed for a middle-aged mama in a muumuu.

Picture this: a sea of handsome, chiseled internet bros in tight t-shirts, each one perfectly caffeinated from their 5 AM gym sessions. By night, they clinked $6,000 bottles of tequila over cigars, swapping stories of how they crushed their latest launch. And then… there was me.

I didn't fit in. At all.

But then, three months later, imagine their shock when I wasn't just in the room—I was sitting at the **golden table.**

See, in this world, income determines seating. And while I started at the back—awkwardly wondering what the heck I was doing there—I had moved to the *front*.

150x in about 7 months – **going from $7k a month to $700k a month and then over $7 million in sales in less than a year**. Lucky number 7.

How? Because I figured out something most people don't: It doesn't matter if you're underestimated. It doesn't matter if you don't fit the mold. It doesn't even matter if you show up looking like someone's eccentric aunt who wandered into the wrong event. *This is your life. Your business. Your rules.*

And that's what this book is about.

Middle-Aged Mama in a Muumuu isn't just a marketing book—it's a no-B.S. playbook for every practitioner, healer, and coach who's been told, "Nope, not you."

For everyone who has doubted whether they could actually make it. For everyone who has watched the so-called experts and thought, *Well, that's great for them, but what about me?* For everyone who has been dismissed, overlooked, or told they're doing it wrong.

This is your permission slip to do it *your* way.

Marketing isn't about fitting in—it's about standing out. And I'm going to show you exactly how to do it.

Let's get to work.

Introduction

The Lucky Few – Entrepreneurs & Healers

Welcome to the Wildest (and Most Fulfilling) Ride of Your Life

So, you decided to start your own practice.

Congratulations, you brave, brilliant, slightly masochistic soul.

Let's be real—running a healthcare practice isn't for the faint of heart. (Or any business, for that matter!) It's like juggling flaming swords while riding a unicycle… blindfolded… on a tightrope… over a pit of hungry alligators.

Because here's what they don't tell you in medical school, nursing school, chiropractic school, or ANY health training college:

Healing people is only half the job.

The other half? Running a business.

And let's be honest—**nobody warned you about that part.**

They taught you anatomy, biochemistry, and diagnostic skills. But where was the class on:

- How to get patients to actually find you?
- How to charge what you're worth (without feeling guilty)?
- How to build a practice that doesn't make you want to run away and live off-grid in a tiny house?

Yeah. That part? **Missing from the curriculum.**

So, if you've ever felt like:

"I'm a great practitioner, but why is running a business SO HARD?"

"Why am I drowning in admin work instead of seeing patients?"

"Why is marketing the most confusing and frustrating thing ever?"

"How do I grow without working myself into the ground?"

Then congratulations—you're in exactly the right place.

The Unique Opportunity We Have in Private Practice Today

We are living in **the best time in history** to be an independent healthcare practitioner.

The demand has never been higher. Patients are waking up to the fact that conventional medicine isn't enough for chronic lifestyle health issues. They're searching for real solutions. **They need you.**

Private practice is on the rise. With telemedicine, online marketing, and direct-pay models, practitioners now have more freedom than ever before. You don't have to be at the mercy of insurance companies.

You have never had more tools at your disposal. From AI-powered marketing to automation tools to scalable revenue streams—you can build a practice **your way.**

But there's a catch…

The marketplace is overflowing with noise. With countless companies fighting for attention, if you don't know how to market yourself effectively, **you'll disappear into the background.**

Patients are more skeptical than ever. We are in a **trust recession** (more on that in a minute). People don't believe claims easily, and they're more cautious about spending money on healthcare.

Most practitioners never learn the business side. That's why so many struggle—or burn out completely.

This book is here to make sure that doesn't happen to you.

Healing + Entrepreneurship: The Most Powerful Combo

You didn't get into healthcare to be a salesperson.

You got into this because you care about people.

- You want to change lives.
- You want to make an impact.
- You want to see patients *truly* heal—not just get another prescription and a "good luck."

But here's the uncomfortable truth:

You cannot help people if they never find you.

You cannot sustain your practice if you don't make money.

You cannot change lives if you're burned out, stressed, and running on fumes.

Marketing and business skills aren't **separate** from being a great practitioner.

They are what **allow you to be a great practitioner—on your terms.**

This book is about learning to thrive in both worlds—as a healer and as an entrepreneur.

Because when you **master business,** you get to practice **the way you want.** It should go without saying but here it is: make sure you follow the scope of practice for your license and follow your local, state, and federal regulations.

- You can choose your ideal patients.
- You can charge what you're worth.
- You can work fewer hours (while making more money).
- You can create financial security for yourself and your family.

And let's be honest—**the more successful you are, the more people you can help.**

This book is your roadmap for making that happen.

The Trust Recession: Why Marketing Is Harder Than Ever (And How to Win Anyway)

If you feel like **patients are harder to sign up than ever, you're not wrong.**

At the time of writing this book – we are living in what's called a **trust recession.**

People are more skeptical. They've been burned by bad doctors, overpriced programs, and false promises. They don't believe marketing claims easily.

What does this mean for you?

It means **you can't rely on dated marketing tricks.**

No generic "we help you feel better" messaging.

No bait-and-switch ads that overpromise and underdeliver.

No assuming that patients will just "trust you" because you're a doctor.

Instead, you must EARN their trust.

Your marketing must be transparent, honest, and educational. You need to nurture relationships before asking for the sale. You have to show proof, build credibility, and communicate in a way that feels human— not corporate.

The good news?

If you do this right, you will stand out immediately.

While other practitioners are still using outdated, trust-destroying marketing, you'll be building relationships, earning credibility, and attracting patients who are excited to work with you.

And that's exactly what you'll learn in this book.

How This Book Will Help You Master Marketing (And Avoid Common Mistakes)

This is **not** a boring theory book.

This is a **real-world, practical, step-by-step guide** to:

Attracting the right patients (no more praying for referrals).

Creating an irresistible offer (so people don't ghost you).

Mastering marketing that actually works (without feeling slimy).

Growing your revenue (without working 80-hour weeks).

Building a practice you LOVE (instead of one that drains you).

Each chapter will give you clear, practical strategies you can implement immediately.

At the end of every chapter, you'll find:

Key Takeaways – The biggest lessons you need to remember.

Action Steps – Simple tasks to help you implement what you've learned.

Pro-Level Tips – Advanced insights to help you get results faster.

Who Is This Book For?

If you're a practitioner who:

- Wants to grow your practice without confusion.
- Hates the idea of "sales" but knows you need to get better at it.

- Feels overwhelmed by marketing but knows it's essential.
- Wants financial freedom—and doesn't want to work 24/7.

Then this book is for you.

Let's Make This Fun

Look, **business books can be boring as heck.**

This one won't be.

We're going to keep it **real, relatable, and actually fun.**

Because if you're going to spend time reading a business book, you might as well enjoy it.

So, are you ready to build the practice of your dreams?

Turn the page. Let's go.

WARNING

You might be tempted to just skip ahead, or cherry pick the information – "*just tell me how to write an ad*" or "*the best method for new patients now*" – right?!?

I advise you go through the book, in order – and **NAIL** every section and then move on to the next one. There's a method to the madness.

Bored talking about your "why"? You probably haven't put the time into it you need to and skip this step, then I *guarantee* you'll be a statistic of an entrepreneur startup practice that failed.

Already think you know your "ideal patient"? I'm *100% certain* no one has ever taught you my "3-Step Ideal Patient Formula". Skip this and you'll wonder why "you're doing everything", but no one responds to your marketing."

Don't want to go over the "5 Money Myths" because "you're good"? Then you'll never realize a truly solid close rate for your no charge consults.

Take the time to work the book – it will transform your practice and it's worth the effort. (That's your "future self" talking there!)

ACTION STEPS

1.Write down your **"why."** Why did you start your practice? What's your bigger mission?

2. Rate yourself from 1-10 on these areas: **Lead Generation, Sales, Admin, Clinical, Leadership.** (Be honest!)

3. **Commit to finishing this book.** Success comes from action—so block out time each week to read and implement.

Next up: Chapter 1—The Why That Drives You.

You're about to dive deep into the **real reason your practice exists—and how to use that to stay motivated, build resilience, and create lasting success.**

Let's do this.

Chapter 1 - The Why That Drives You

Why Your "Why" Matters More Than Anything Else

Let's start with a simple but critical question:

Why did you start your practice?

Not just the surface-level answer. Not just "*I wanted to help people.*"

I mean the *real* reason—the one that gets you out of bed in the morning even when you're exhausted, frustrated, or wondering if it would be easier to quit and get a job at Target.

- What is the bigger mission that fuels you?
- What impact do you want to make on the world?
- What kind of life do you want for yourself and your family?

If your answer is **fuzzy, weak, or purely about money**, we need to fix that.

Because your "why" is what keeps you going when things get hard.

And things will get hard.

Running a private practice isn't all smooth sailing. It's late nights, tough decisions, financial stress, and moments where you question your sanity.

But when your "why" is clear, strong, and deeply personal— you'll push through.

A weak "why" leads to burnout and failure.

A strong "why" makes you unstoppable.

Let's make yours bulletproof.

The 5 D's: The Mindset of a Thriving Practice Owner

Success in private practice isn't just about clinical skills.

It's about mindset, resilience, and knowing how to push forward even when you don't feel like it.

The most successful practice owners have five key traits that set them apart. I call them **The 5 D's:**

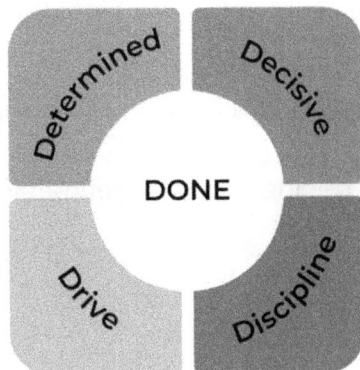

1. Determination – The ability to keep going when things get tough

When a patient ghosts you.

When a launch flops.

When an ad campaign doesn't work.

When you second-guess your entire existence.

Do you let these setbacks stop you, or do you keep moving forward?

2. Decisiveness – Making choices quickly and moving forward

Successful practice owners don't get stuck in analysis paralysis.

They make a decision, take action, and adjust as needed.

- Should I do social media or email marketing?
- Should I price my program at $497 or $4997?
- Should I hire a VA (virtual assistant) now or wait?

The wrong move? Sitting on the decision for six months.

Successful owners decide, act, and refine along the way.

3. Driven – Internal motivation that keeps you going

No one is coming to save you.

No one is going to wake you up in the morning and say:

- "Hey, you should post that marketing video today!"
- "Hey, it's time to follow up with those leads!"
- "Hey, it's time to raise your prices!"

You have to be your own biggest motivator.

If you're waiting for the perfect moment, the perfect mood, or someone to push you… you're already behind.

4. Discipline – Doing the work even when you don't feel like it

Motivation comes and goes.

Discipline is what keeps you on track.

- You don't feel like working out—but you do it anyway.
- You don't feel like writing marketing emails—but you do it anyway.
- You don't feel like showing up online—but you do it anyway.

Discipline is the **difference** between practitioners who make it and those who don't.

5. Done – Taking action instead of overthinking

The number one killer of practice growth?

Overthinking.

- "But what if my website isn't perfect yet?"
- "But what if my messaging isn't 100% right?"
- "But what if people don't like my social media posts?"

Stop waiting for perfection.

Done is better than perfect.

When cash flow is tight...

When you're frustrated with marketing...

Your mission is what keeps you moving.

Too many practitioners lose sight of why they started—and that's when burnout creeps in.

- Are you prioritizing the parts of your practice that bring you joy?
- Are you setting boundaries, so you don't burn out?
- Are you still connected to the passion that started this journey?

Your job isn't just to heal others—it's to build a practice that supports you, too.

Let's make sure you don't lose sight of that.

Because when you put in the effort to make this work, you not only help a lot of patients along the way – but you'll also create the **most amazing life** you can only *dream* of at this point.

I'm in the business of making dreams a reality. Let's do this.

Chin Whiskers, Belly Bloat & The Million Reasons to Quit Before You Even Start

Listen, there are about a *million* reasons why you could talk yourself out of building your dream business before you even start. I know, because I had them all.

- **Menopause brain**—which means I could remember every embarrassing thing I did in middle school but not why I walked into a room.

- **Internet trolls**—people who have *never* built a business but somehow *know* yours won't work.

- **The unavoidable battle with humidity**—because nothing says *professional* like looking like you got electrocuted before filming a video.

- **The sheer audacity of belly bloat**—you eat one grain of rice, and suddenly your stomach thinks it's starring in its own pregnancy announcement.

- **And let's not forget chin whiskers.** I don't know *when* it started, but at some point, I became part-cat.

And yet, despite *all* of that, here I am. *And here you are.*

So, the real question isn't *why you can't do this.* It's **why you absolutely have to.**

What is the thing that's going to keep you going even on the days when you feel like throwing your laptop into the ocean and moving to a goat farm?

Because that's the thing that will carry you through *every* challenge—through the self-doubt, the bad hair days, and the internet strangers who think your pricing is outrageous (but will drop $12 on a green juice without blinking).

Your *why* must be bigger than your fears. Bigger than the setbacks. Bigger than the voice in your head telling you it's safer to stay small.

So, find it. Name it. And let's get to work. Because if a middle-aged mama in a muumuu can build a business that skyrockets to success, *so can you.*

ACTION STEPS – Clarifying Your Practice's Mission

1. Write down your "why."

- What is your bigger mission beyond just "helping people"?
- What kind of impact do you want to make?
- What kind of life do you want for yourself?

2. PRO TIP: Fill out my detailed "Find Your Why" handout. It's worth spending the time answering the questions (in order) and really thinking through each one. Here you go:

- What is it you want to change?

- What is it you want instead?

- Why do you want this?

- What would your life be like if you made this change?

- What do you think would happen if you don't create this change?

- What's the best you could imagine feeling?

- What would be possible in your life with this change? Dream big.

- How will you handle those that criticize you or attempt to derail your efforts?

- What's your plan if you experience challenges/bumps along the way?

- What do you want your current motivated self to tell your future self to keep you going when you feel tired, worn-out, bored, impatient, frustrated…what do you want to remember to keep you going?

- Do you believe you are worthy of this change? What's the kindest, most loving message you can say to yourself?

3. Rate yourself from 1-10 on the 5 D's:

- **Determination** (Do I push forward when things get tough?)

- **Decisiveness** (Do I make quick decisions and take action?)

- **Driven** (Am I self-motivated to grow my business?)

- **Discipline** (Do I follow through even when I don't feel like it?)

- **Done** (Do I understand what it takes to move a project forward?)

4. Set a reminder to revisit your "why" every month.

- Burnout happens when you forget why you started.

- Keep your mission front and center.

5. Make one decision you've been putting off.

- What's something you've been overthinking?

- Decide. Act. Move forward.

Next Up: Chapter 2 – The Climb Higher Board Game

Now that you're clear on your why, it's time to talk strategy.

- Where are you in your practice growth?

- What level are you climbing toward?

- What moves should you be making right now?

Let's map out your game plan.

Turn the page. Let's go.

Chapter 2 - Climb Higher: The Practice Growth Game

How to Think Like a Business Owner, Beyond a Healer

You didn't start your practice to be a **marketer, accountant, or operations manager**—you started it because you wanted to **help people**. You wanted to change lives, practice real healthcare, and feel fulfilled in your work.

And yet…

Here you are, **drowning in admin**, constantly **trying to get new patients**, and wondering **why your schedule isn't as full as it should be**.

Because **being a great healer** isn't enough.

The difference between a struggling practitioner and a successful practice owner **isn't just skill—it's strategy.**

There are two types of practitioners:

- The ones who focus **only on their clinical skills** and hope the patients will come.
- The ones who understand that **business is a game**— and learn how to play it.

If you want to grow a profitable, sustainable, stress-free practice, you must stop thinking like just a practitioner and start thinking like a business owner.

That means:

Understanding how patients find and choose you.

Learning how to price, package, and present your services.

Building a predictable way to attract leads—instead of relying on word-of-mouth.

Running your practice with systems, not chaos.

You don't have to love business. But if you don't at least respect it, it will run you into the ground.

Why You Need a Strategy (Not Just More Hustle)

Most practitioners try to grow by **working harder** instead of **working smarter**.

"If I just see more patients, my practice will grow."

"If I just post more on social media, I'll get more leads."

"If I just lower my prices, more people will sign up."

But **that's not how growth works**.

Growth isn't about working more hours or grinding yourself into exhaustion. It's about playing the right game—and making the right moves at the right time.

The most successful practitioners don't just work harder—they work on the right things.

The problem? Most practitioners **don't know** what the right things are—so they waste time, energy, and money doing everything instead of focusing on the next best move for their practice.

This is where The Climb Higher Board Game comes in.

How the Climb Higher Board Game Works

Imagine business growth as a game—where each move you make builds on the last one.

There are steps, levels, and strategies that allow you to climb higher without spinning your wheels.

This is NOT about:

Random marketing tactics

Hustling endlessly

Trying to do everything all at once

Instead, it's about making strategic moves—and making sure you're focusing on the right things at the right time.

Think of your business like a board game:

- You **start at the bottom**, building the foundation.
- You **move strategically**, step by step, making decisions that **set you up for future success**.
- Every **wrong move** (or skipping steps) slows you down—or even sends you back a few spaces.
- The goal? **To build a thriving, profitable, sustainable practice—without burnout.**

Common Mistakes Practitioners Make When Trying to Grow

Skipping steps – Trying to "scale" before you even have a steady flow of patients.

Focusing on the wrong things – Spending hours on social media instead of fixing your offer.

Throwing money at ads before you're ready – Running ads without first having a strategy in place.

Believing more work = more success – Burning yourself out without actually making more money.

If you've been **feeling stuck**, frustrated, or exhausted... it's probably because you've been playing the game **without a strategy**.

ACTION STEPS: Mapping Your Personal Growth Path

Let's get clear on **where you are now**—so you can make your next move strategically.

1. **Identify where you feel stuck.**

   - Are you struggling to get new patients?
   - Do you have plenty of leads, but they aren't converting?
   - Are you working too many hours but not making enough?

2. **Define what growth means to you.**

   - Do you want more revenue?
   - More time freedom?
   - A bigger impact?

3. **Choose ONE focus area for the next 90 days.**

- Don't try to "fix everything" at once.

- Pick ONE area (lead generation, pricing, systems, sales, etc.) and commit to improving it.

Next Up: The 3x10 Approach – Finding Your Best Business Model

Now that you understand **the importance of playing the right game**, it's time to figure out **what kind of practice YOU want to build**.

In the next chapter, we'll break down:

The **3 practice levels** – Operator, Manager, Founder

The **10 practice models** – and which one fits YOU best

How to **avoid the mistake of building a business that doesn't fit your life**

Because **building the wrong kind of practice** is just as bad as **not growing at all**.

Let's make sure you're on the right path.

PS – yes – this is a marketing book. Yes, I will "get to it" soon. Yes, you must read all of this and do the action steps, or you won't be ready for the marketing.

PPS – irritated? Touch tushy. Practice some discipline and muscle through it. Read it in the bath or while getting a pedicure...I don't care – I'm not above being bathroom reading material. All I care about is that you read it, so YOU ARE READY to crush it.

You can do this.

Chapter 3 - The 3x10 Approach

The Biggest Business Decision You'll Ever Make

Imagine this:

You start your practice, eager to help people, and things are going great. Patients love you. You're busy. But then, somewhere around year two or three, you wake up in a cold sweat thinking…

"Oh crap. I built the wrong business."

Your schedule is packed, but you're exhausted. You're either making great money but never seeing your family, or you're working way too hard for way too little.

Here's the secret no one tells you:

It's not enough to just "start a practice." You must start the **right** practice—one that matches how you actually want to live.

- If you don't choose the right level, you'll be disappointed or feeling the grind.
- If you don't choose the right model, you'll build a business you hate.

So, let's make sure you get it **right**—before you find yourself accidentally running a business that makes you miserable.

The 3 Practice Levels: Operator, Manager, Founder

Each level has different rewards, different challenges, and different rules.

3 Practice Levels

1. Operator
$200k-$500k per year, solo-practitioner, no staff or 1 virtual assistant or front desk staff, up to $750k with health coach

2. Manager
$600k-$3M per year, multi-practitioner, owner marketing for all, lots of mgmt, easiest place for biz bloat, high cost/lower profit margin, stressful

3. Founder
$2M-$10M+ per year, 1 offer & CSM model with renewal or MRR, build strong silo with scalable marketing, maintain solid profit margin, build sales team, wealth builder

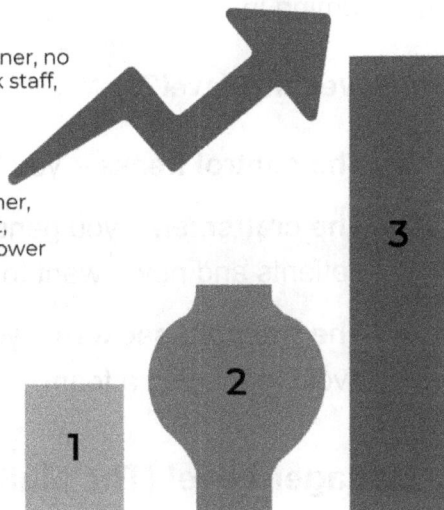

1. Operator Level (The Technician)

- **You are the business.** You see the patients, handle the marketing, and make all the decisions.

- **Great for control freaks.** If you like knowing everything is done your way, this level works.

- **Low overhead.** You don't need a huge team or a massive facility.

Earnings Potential: $200,000 – $500,000 per year (or up to $750,000 with a health coach).

Best Practice Models: Fee-for-Service, Program-Based, Health Coaching, Mobile Medical Services.

Biggest Risk: You're trapped. If you stop working, the money stops coming in.

Who loves this level?

- **The control freaks** – you like doing things your way.

- **The craftsmen** – you genuinely love working with patients and never want to stop.

- **The freedom seekers** – you want to work solo and avoid managing a team.

2. Manager Level (The Multi-Practitioner Boss)

- **You run a team.** Other practitioners help serve patients so you're not doing it all alone.

- **Scalability.** You make money even when you're not in the office.

- **You're not responsible for everything.** Admins, coaches, and other practitioners keep things moving.

Earnings Potential: $600,000 – $3,000,000 per year. (but you are sharing it with a team)

Best Practice Models: Membership Model, Direct Primary Care (DPC), Program-Based (Scaled), Medical Spa, Retail Establishment.

Biggest Risk: You have more overhead, and now you're responsible for managing people.

Who loves this level?

- **The natural leaders** – you love mentoring and building a team.

- **The system-builders** – you love creating workflows and streamlining operations.

- **The big-picture thinkers** – you'd rather work on your business than in it.

3. Founder Level (The CEO & Empire Builder)

- **You don't see patients anymore** (or just select/exclusive level). Your business runs without you.

- **Massive impact.** You help thousands of people through scale.

- **Financial freedom.** Your income isn't tied to the hours you work.

Earnings Potential: $2,000,000 – $10,000,000+ per year.

Best Practice Models: Medical-Connected Brand, Scaled Membership, Scaled Program-Based, Concierge Care (Premium Tier), Franchised Medical Spa.

Biggest Risk: It's all about marketing, branding, and leadership. If you hate those things, you'll struggle.

Who loves this level?

- **The visionaries** – you're always thinking 10 years ahead.

- **The entrepreneurs** – you love marketing, branding, and building something huge.

- **The legacy builders** – you want to create something that outlives you.

The 10 Practice Models: Choose Your Path Wisely

Now that you know the level you want, it's time to choose the right business model.

Why this matters:

- If you pick the wrong model, it's painful to switch.

- Your daily life *depends* on the model you choose.

- Some models scale easily. Others don't.

1. Fee-for-Service Model

Overview

The fee-for-service model operates on a straightforward transactional basis: patients pay for each visit or service at the time it is provided. This approach allows flexibility in pricing and service delivery, making it a common choice for practitioners who are just starting out or prefer not to be tied to long-term patient commitments.

Typical Day in the Life

- **Morning:** See 5-6 patients for various concerns such as acute issues, wellness checkups, or chronic illness management.

- **Afternoon:** Review patient charts, follow up on lab results, and conduct another 5-6 patient visits.

- **Evening:** Complete administrative tasks such as billing, patient communication, and scheduling for the next day.

Staffing Requirements

- **Essential Staff:** Front desk personnel for scheduling, check-ins, and processing payments.

- **Optional:** Medical assistant or nurse to assist with vitals, charting, or basic clinical tasks.

- **Technology:** EMR software to streamline patient documentation and billing.

Patient Visit Volume

- Average of **10-15 patients per day**, depending on appointment length and complexity. (Some have to do high volume because they undercharge and overstaff – don't recommend that!)

Marketing Needs

- **Level:** Moderate. Fee-for-service practices rely on a steady stream of new patients to sustain revenue.

- **Key Strategies:** Local SEO, Google Ads, patient referral programs, and establishing relationships with other local healthcare providers.

Typical Legal Setup and Concerns

- **Legal Entity:** Sole proprietorship, LLC, or S-Corp are common structures. LLCs are particularly popular for liability protection.

- **Compliance:** Ensure you meet state and federal regulations for healthcare practices, including HIPAA for patient data privacy.

- **Contracts:** Consider liability waivers and clear service agreements to set expectations for payment and care.

Typical Earnings

- **Range:** $150,000 to $400,000 annually, depending on patient volume, pricing, and overhead.

- **Factors:** Earnings depend on location, specialization, and operational efficiency. Higher-volume practices in urban areas often see higher revenue.

Pros

- **Flexibility:** Set your own pricing and services without long-term commitments.

- **Simplicity:** Easy to understand for both patients and practitioners.

- **Scalability:** Potential for high patient volume.

- **Predictable Payments:** Immediate revenue from services rendered.

Cons

- **High Marketing Needs:** Requires a steady flow of new patients.

- **Volume Pressure:** Income depends on seeing more patients, which may lead to burnout.

- **Limited Patient Retention:** No built-in structure for long-term engagement.

- **Administrative Burden:** Requires constant billing and follow-up for payment if using insurance, or patients more likely to drop off if cash-based because no commitment and forced to make a financial decision for every visit.

2. Program-Based Model

Overview

In a program-based model, practitioners offer patients comprehensive care plans that span several months. These packages often include a mix of one-on-one visits, educational materials, group coaching, and supplemental products like meal plans or lab tests. This model emphasizes patient outcomes over individual appointments, making it ideal for addressing chronic issues or specific health goals.

Typical Day in the Life

- **Morning:** Conduct 2-3 in-depth patient sessions to discuss progress, adjust protocols, and provide coaching.

- **Afternoon:** Host group coaching calls or webinars for program participants, develop educational materials, and review patient updates.

- **Evening:** Follow up with patients via email or portal, and collaborate with team members to enhance program delivery.

Staffing Requirements

- **Core Team:** Health coach or nutritionist to provide additional patient support.

- Administrative staff to handle enrollment, scheduling, and payments.

- **Optional:** Marketing specialist to create and manage campaigns.

Patient Visit Volume

- Typically, **2-5 individual patient visits per day**, supplemented by group sessions and digital communication. (or do 6-10 in a day and work less days – I recommend only 2 patient-facing days per week).

- Lower daily volume compared to fee-for-service, but revenue is often higher due to program value pricing.

Marketing Needs

- **Level:** High. Success depends on attracting patients who are ready to commit to long-term solutions.

- **Key Strategies:** Social media advertising, webinars, email funnels, and partnerships with influencers or local businesses.

Typical Legal Setup and Concerns

- **Legal Entity:** LLC or S-Corp for liability protection and tax benefits.

- **Contracts:** Detailed agreements outlining program terms, refund policies, and scope of care. Ensure patients understand what is and isn't included. Often require a PPC (patient maintains a Primary Care Physician relationship and care).

- **Regulations:** Compliance with advertising laws, particularly for claims about health outcomes. Include disclaimers where necessary.

Typical Earnings

- **Range:** $200,000 to $600,000 annually, depending on program pricing, enrollment volume, and operational costs.
- **Factors:** Programs priced between $2,000 and $10,000 can yield significant revenue with fewer patients compared to fee-for-service models. Practitioners with strong marketing systems tend to scale more quickly.

Pros

- **Higher Revenue Potential:** Programs typically command higher prices.
- **Improved Outcomes:** Focus on long-term goals often leads to better patient results.
- **Efficient Scheduling:** Lower daily patient volume compared to fee-for-service.
- **Predictable Income:** Prepaid programs provide consistent cash flow.

Cons

- **High Marketing Demand:** Attracting patients willing to invest in programs takes effort.
- **Complex Setup:** Requires planning, structuring, and maintaining program materials.

- **Risk of Refunds:** Patients may request refunds if expectations aren't met.

- **Patient Expectations:** High investment leads to higher expectations for results.

3. Membership Model

Overview

The membership model involves patients paying a recurring monthly or annual fee for access to a predefined set of services. Additional services can often be purchased a la carte, creating flexibility and predictable income for the practice. This model fosters patient retention and loyalty while providing consistent revenue streams.

Typical Day in the Life

- **Morning:** Conduct 4-5 wellness consultations or routine visits with members.

- **Afternoon:** Deliver group education sessions or workshops tailored to member needs.

- **Evening:** Review member inquiries through a patient portal and plan upcoming group events or services.

Staffing Requirements

- **Core Team:** Administrative staff to manage memberships, billing, and inquiries.

- Practitioner(s) to provide services covered in the membership.

- **Optional:** Health coaches or wellness specialists to expand the range of included services.

Patient Visit Volume

- Average of **4-6 visits per day**, supplemented by group sessions and a flexible schedule to address member needs.

Marketing Needs

- **Level:** Moderate to High. Effective marketing is essential to attract and retain members.

- **Key Strategies:**

- Referral programs and testimonials to build trust.

- Educational content and community-building on social platforms.

Typical Legal Setup and Concerns

- **Legal Entity:** LLC or S-Corp to minimize liability and optimize tax benefits.

- **Compliance:** Ensure services comply with state and federal guidelines for membership-based practices. Clearly outline membership terms and limitations in contracts.

- **Contracts:** Membership agreements must define what services are included, the scope of care, and cancellation policies.

Typical Earnings

- **Range:** $150,000 to $500,000 annually, depending on membership size and pricing structure.

- **Factors:** Steady recurring revenue grows with strong retention efforts and member satisfaction. Practices that offer high-value extras can charge premium rates.

Pros

- **Recurring Revenue:** Predictable income through monthly or annual fees.

- **Patient Retention:** Encourages long-term relationships.

- **Flexibility:** Allows customization of included services.

- **Lower Patient Volume:** Fewer daily appointments needed compared to other models.

Cons

- **Churn Risk:** Retaining members requires consistent engagement and satisfaction.

- **Marketing Intensive:** Requires continuous outreach to build and sustain membership.

- **Limited Scalability:** Growth depends on expanding membership capacity.

- **Complex Management:** Membership billing and tracking can be challenging.

4. Direct Primary Care (DPC)

Overview

Direct Primary Care is a membership-based model specifically for primary care services. Patients pay a monthly fee in exchange for unrestricted access to routine and preventive care, often bypassing traditional insurance. This model emphasizes patient-centered care and simplicity in billing.

Typical Day in the Life

- **Morning:** Provide comprehensive care for 4-5 patients, addressing acute issues or preventive needs.

- **Afternoon:** Review diagnostic results, conduct follow-ups, and document care plans.

- **Evening:** Respond to patient inquiries through messaging platforms and ensure continuity of care.

Staffing Requirements

- **Core Team:** Minimal staff required: A medical assistant or nurse can assist with basic clinical and administrative tasks.

- Practitioner handles most patient interactions and decisions.

Patient Visit Volume

- Typically, **4-8 patients per day** (can be higher), with extended appointment times to allow for personalized care.

- Lower daily volume compared to insurance-based models, but the focus is on quality over quantity.

Marketing Needs

- **Level:** Moderate. DPC practices rely on demonstrating value to patients who seek a more personalized experience.

- **Key Strategies:**

- Community outreach and partnerships.

- Transparent pricing and educational campaigns about DPC benefits.

Typical Legal Setup and Concerns

- **Legal Entity:** LLC or S-Corp for liability protection and operational efficiency.

- **Compliance:** DPC practices must adhere to state laws regarding direct care agreements. Some states have specific DPC regulations.

- **Contracts:** Patient agreements should clearly define the scope of care, monthly fees, and services covered.

Typical Earnings

- **Range:** $120,000 to $300,000 annually, depending on patient panel size and pricing. (Can be earn more with higher volume)

- **Factors:** DPC practices with higher patient retention and moderately priced memberships often see steady growth. Practitioners may adjust fees based on local market demand.

Pros

- **Patient-Centered Care:** Offers more time for each patient.

- **Simplified Billing:** Avoids insurance complexities.

- **Steady Revenue:** Recurring monthly fees ensure predictable income.

- **High Satisfaction:** Patients appreciate the personalized care.

Cons

- **Limited Patient Panel:** May cap earnings unless fees are high.

- **Legal Considerations:** State-specific regulations may complicate setup.

- **Marketing Needs:** Requires education about DPC benefits to attract patients.

- **Initial Investment:** Building a patient panel can take time.

5. Concierge Care

Overview

Concierge care offers an elevated level of service at a premium price. Patients pay a high annual or monthly fee for personalized, on-demand access to their provider. This model is ideal for practitioners who want to focus on fewer patients and deliver exceptional, tailored care.

Typical Day in the Life

- **Morning:** Meet with 2-3 patients for detailed consultations or wellness reviews.

- **Afternoon:** Coordinate specialist referrals, proactive follow-ups, and personalized care plans.

- **Evening:** Remain on-call for urgent concerns or conduct home visits as needed.

Staffing Requirements

- **Core Team:** Administrative staff to manage schedules, patient communication, and memberships.

- **Optional**: A nurse or medical assistant for clinical support.

- **Optional Additions:** Nutritionists, wellness coaches, or concierge coordinators to enhance services.

Patient Visit Volume

- Average of **2-4 visits per day**, focusing on quality and depth of care rather than volume.

Marketing Needs

- **Level:** Low to Moderate. Exclusivity and high-touch service often attract word-of-mouth referrals.

- **Key Strategies:**

- Highlighting premium services and testimonials.

- Networking with high-income communities and business professionals.

Typical Legal Setup and Concerns

- **Legal Entity:** LLC or S-Corp is preferred for liability protection and scalability.

- **Compliance:** Ensure compliance with state laws on concierge medicine, particularly regarding billing transparency and contractual obligations.

- **Contracts:** Clear patient agreements outlining services, costs, and limitations to avoid misunderstandings.

Typical Earnings

- **Range:** $250,000 to $750,000 annually, depending on membership fees and patient panel size.

- **Factors:** Earnings are influenced by location, the exclusivity of services, and the ability to deliver exceptional patient experiences.

Pros

- **Premium Revenue:** Higher fees lead to significant income potential.

- **High Satisfaction:** Patients value VIP-level access and care.

- **Lower Patient Volume:** Focus on quality over quantity.

- **Strong Relationships:** Deep connections with a smaller patient base.

Cons

- **Exclusive Market:** Limited to high-income patients, narrowing the target audience.

- **Availability Pressure:** May require being on-call frequently.

- **Marketing Challenges:** Establishing exclusivity takes time and effort.

- **Ethical Perception:** Can be viewed as elitist or inaccessible.

6. Health Coaching

Overview

Health coaching focuses on guiding clients toward achieving wellness goals through education, motivation, and accountability. It does not involve direct medical care and is perfect for practitioners passionate about lifestyle interventions and holistic health.

Typical Day in the Life

- **Morning:** Conduct 3-4 coaching sessions focusing on nutrition, exercise, or habit-building.
- **Afternoon:** Develop content, create meal plans, or design educational resources for clients.
- **Evening:** Follow up with clients via email or a digital platform, and plan for upcoming sessions.

Staffing Requirements

- **Core Team:** Often a solo practice with no additional staff.
- **Optional**: Virtual assistants or social media managers for marketing support.

Patient Visit Volume

- Average of **3-5 sessions per day**, with significant flexibility in scheduling.

Marketing Needs

- **Level:** High. Building a personal brand and maintaining a strong online presence are critical.
- **Key Strategies:**

- Social media campaigns, content marketing, and email funnels.

- Hosting workshops or webinars to attract potential clients.

Typical Legal Setup and Concerns

- **Legal Entity:** LLC is common for liability protection.

- **Compliance:** Avoid offering medical advice unless properly credentialed; focus on education and guidance.

- **Contracts:** Coaching agreements should clearly outline services, limitations, and payment terms.

Typical Earnings

- **Range:** $50,000 to $150,000 annually if follow typical health coaching model, with potential for growth through digital products or group coaching high 6- or 7-figure practice growth using our model.

- **Factors:** Income varies widely based on pricing, client volume, and additional revenue streams such as online courses or retreats.

Pros

- **Low Overhead:** Minimal setup costs compared to medical practices.

- **Flexibility:** Ability to work remotely and customize offerings.

- **Scalable:** Opportunity to expand through group coaching or digital products.

- **Focus on Prevention:** Helps clients improve lifestyle and avoid chronic diseases.

Cons

- **Lower Income Potential:** Revenue is typically lower than medical models.

- **Marketing-Intensive:** Requires a strong personal brand to attract clients.

- **Legal Restrictions:** Cannot provide medical advice without proper credentials.

- **Inconsistent Revenue:** Client retention may be a challenge.

7. Medical Spa

Overview

Medical spas combine traditional spa services with medical treatments, offering clients aesthetic procedures like Botox, fillers, laser treatments, and skin rejuvenation. These practices operate in a brick-and-mortar setting and require licensed medical professionals to oversee or perform treatments.

Typical Day in the Life

- **Morning:** Perform 4-5 aesthetic treatments, such as injectables or laser procedures.

- **Afternoon:** Conduct consultations for new clients, provide skincare education, and perform follow-up treatments.
- **Evening:** Restock supplies, review sales, and meet with the team to discuss promotions or client feedback.

Staffing Requirements

- **Core Team:** Licensed medical professionals (e.g., nurse practitioners, physician assistants, or doctors) for treatments.
- Aesthetic technicians or estheticians for non-medical services.
- Front desk staff to manage scheduling and payments.
- **Optional Additions:** Marketing or sales staff to drive customer acquisition.

Patient Visit Volume

- Typically **8-15 appointments per day**, depending on service types and appointment length.

Marketing Needs

- **Level:** High. Competitive markets require robust marketing strategies to attract new clients.
- **Key Strategies:**
- Social media promotions, especially before-and-after photos.
- Partnerships with influencers or local businesses.

- Targeted ads and SEO for aesthetic services.

Typical Legal Setup and Concerns

- **Legal Entity:** LLC or S-Corp for liability protection.
- **Compliance:** Adherence to state regulations on aesthetic procedures, medical oversight, and licensing.
- **Contracts:** Consent forms for all procedures, along with clear refund and cancellation policies.

Typical Earnings

- **Range:** $250,000 to $1,000,000+ annually, depending on location, services offered, and patient volume.
- **Factors:** High-margin services like injectables contribute significantly to profitability.

Pros

- **High Revenue Potential:** Aesthetic services are often high-margin.
- **Growing Demand:** Popular and expanding market.
- **Upselling Opportunities:** Cross-sell treatments and skincare products.
- **Brand Building:** Opportunity to establish a luxury brand.

Cons

- **High Startup Costs:** Requires investment in equipment and staff.

- **Regulatory Compliance:** Strict licensing and oversight for medical treatments.

- **Competitive Market:** Success depends on strong marketing and differentiation.

- **Staff Turnover:** Retaining skilled professionals can be challenging.

8. Mobile Medical Services

Overview

Mobile medical services bring healthcare directly to patients' homes, workplaces, or community centers. This model offers convenience and accessibility, with services ranging from urgent care to wellness visits or vaccinations.

Typical Day in the Life

- **Morning:** Travel to a patient's home to provide a wellness checkup or vaccination.

- **Afternoon:** Visit workplaces or community events for health screenings.

- **Evening:** Restock supplies, organize records, and prepare for the next day's appointments.

Staffing Requirements

- **Core Team:** Licensed medical professionals to deliver services.

- Driver or logistical support for transportation and supply management.

- **Optional Additions:** Administrative staff to handle scheduling and patient communication remotely.

Patient Visit Volume

- Typically **3-6 visits per day**, depending on travel time and service complexity.

Marketing Needs

- **Level:** Moderate. Effective outreach focuses on convenience and personalized care.

- **Key Strategies:**

- Local advertising and SEO for mobile services.

- Partnerships with businesses and community organizations.

Typical Legal Setup and Concerns

- **Legal Entity:** LLC or S-Corp for liability protection.

- **Compliance:** Adherence to state and federal regulations regarding mobile healthcare. Ensure proper handling and transportation of medical supplies.

- **Contracts:** Service agreements defining the scope of care and payment terms.

Typical Earnings

- **Range:** $100,000 to $400,000 annually, depending on services offered and patient volume.

- **Factors:** Revenue depends on the efficiency of logistics and ability to scale operations.

Pros

- **Convenience:** Patients appreciate care brought to their location.

- **Low Overhead:** Avoids the costs of maintaining a physical office.

- **Flexible Services:** Adaptable to various needs, from vaccinations to wellness checks.

- **Underserved Markets:** Can reach patients in rural or underserved areas.

Cons

- **Logistical Challenges:** Requires careful planning for travel and supplies.

- **Lower Patient Volume:** Travel time limits the number of daily appointments.

- **Marketing Effort:** Patients need to be educated about mobile services.

- **Regulatory Hurdles:** Compliance with mobile healthcare laws is essential.

9. Retail Establishment

Overview

Retail establishments, such as pharmacies, supplement shops, or wellness boutiques, provide healthcare-related products and services directly to customers. These practices focus on a brick-and-mortar setup with a significant emphasis on product sales and customer education.

Typical Day in the Life

- **Morning:** Open the establishment, check inventory, and prepare for customer traffic.

- **Afternoon:** Assist customers with product selection, answer health-related questions, and provide education on supplements or wellness products.

- **Evening:** Restock shelves, track sales, and prepare for the next day's operations.

Staffing Requirements

- **Core Team:** Sales associates with knowledge of wellness products.

- Licensed professionals (pharmacists, nutritionists, or naturopaths) for consultations or recommendations.

- Administrative staff for inventory management and bookkeeping.

Patient Visit Volume

- **Varies:** Depends on foot traffic and customer demand, ranging from 20-100 customers daily in busy locations.

Marketing Needs

- **Level:** High. Attracting customers requires consistent promotions and visibility.
- **Key Strategies:**
- Local advertising and social media campaigns.
- Loyalty programs and discounts to encourage repeat business.
- Hosting in-store events or workshops.

Typical Legal Setup and Concerns

- **Legal Entity:** LLC or S-Corp to protect against liability and streamline tax benefits.
- **Compliance:** Adherence to retail regulations, including labeling, sales tax, and, if applicable, licensing for selling supplements or medications.
- **Contracts:** Supplier agreements and vendor contracts for product inventory.

Typical Earnings

- **Range:** $200,000 to $800,000 annually, depending on location, product pricing, and customer volume.
- **Factors:** Revenue depends heavily on product margins, effective marketing, and foot traffic.

Pros

- **Diverse Revenue Streams:** Earn from product sales and consultations.

- **Customer Engagement:** Frequent foot traffic builds brand loyalty.

- **Scalable:** Potential to expand to multiple locations.

- **Community Presence:** Establishes a local hub for wellness.

Cons

- **High Overhead:** Rent, inventory, and staffing costs can be significant.

- **Market Dependence:** Revenue relies heavily on location and customer demand.

- **Inventory Risks:** Overstock or expired products can reduce profitability.

- **Operational Complexity:** Requires strong management systems.

10. Medical-Connected Brand

Overview

Medical-connected brands focus on developing a strong identity through products, services, or digital offerings. Examples include selling medical devices, creating online education platforms, or building a personal brand around medical expertise.

Typical Day in the Life

- **Morning:** Develop content for online platforms, such as webinars, blog posts, or social media.
- **Afternoon:** Manage product development, customer service, and collaborations with other brands or influencers.
- **Evening:** Analyze sales data, refine marketing strategies, and plan for upcoming campaigns.

Staffing Requirements

- **Core Team:** Marketing specialists for brand visibility and campaign execution.
- Product developers or content creators to expand offerings.
- Customer support for inquiries and troubleshooting.

Patient Visit Volume

- **None:** Revenue is not dependent on direct patient visits but rather on product or service sales.

Marketing Needs

- **Level:** Very High. Building a recognizable brand requires continuous marketing and innovation.
- **Key Strategies:**

- Paid advertising and influencer partnerships.

- Affiliate marketing and collaborations.

Typical Legal Setup and Concerns

- **Legal Entity:** LLC or S-Corp for liability protection and tax advantages.

- **Compliance:** Ensure compliance with consumer protection laws, FDA regulations for medical devices (if applicable), and advertising standards.

- **Contracts:** Clear terms of service, licensing agreements (if applicable), and contracts with affiliates or influencers.

Typical Earnings

- **Range:** $100,000 to $2,000,000+ annually, depending on product pricing, market reach, and scalability.

- **Factors:** Earnings are heavily influenced by marketing effectiveness, brand reputation, and the ability to scale digital or product-based offerings efficiently.

Pros

- **Scalability:** Digital products or devices can reach a global audience.

- **Passive Income Potential:** Once established, offers ongoing revenue with minimal effort.

- **Flexibility:** Operate from anywhere with an internet connection.

- **Brand Authority:** Builds a reputation as a leader in your niche.

Cons

- **High Marketing Needs:** Success depends on consistent visibility and brand building.

- **Upfront Investment:** Product development and marketing can be costly.

- **Competition:** Saturated markets may require significant differentiation.

- **Regulatory Compliance:** Complex rules for advertising and selling medical-related products.

Here's how the **10 practice models** fit into the 3 levels:

Best Models for Operator Level

- **Fee-for-Service** – The classic. You charge per visit. Simple, predictable, but requires constant marketing.

- **Program-Based** – Sell structured care plans instead of one-off visits. More revenue per patient, better outcomes.

- **Health Coaching** – Low overhead, works well online, but lower revenue unless you scale with group programs.

- **Mobile Medical Services** – Bring care directly to patients. Flexible but hard to scale.

Best Models for Manager Level

- **Membership Model** – Patients pay monthly, giving you predictable income.

- **Direct Primary Care (DPC)** – A membership model specifically for primary care.

- **Program-Based (Scaled)** – More group coaching, fewer one-on-one visits.

- **Medical Spa** – High-margin services like Botox, IV therapy, and skin rejuvenation.

- **Retail Establishment** – A wellness store with consultations on the side.

Best Models for Founder Level

- **Medical-Connected Brand** – Selling supplements, courses, or digital products instead of direct patient care.

- **Scaled Membership** – A multi-location or national membership model.

- **Scaled Program-Based** – Group programs that scale beyond one-on-one work.

- **Concierge Care (Premium Tier)** – High-ticket, VIP-style care.

- **Franchised Medical Spa** – Scaling a successful aesthetic practice into multiple locations.

How to Avoid the Biggest Mistake

The biggest mistake practitioners make?

They build a practice model that **doesn't match** their personality or goals.

I've seen it happen so many times:

- A practitioner loves patient care but accidentally builds a Manager-level business… and hates managing people.

- Someone dreams of Founder-level freedom but keeps using Operator strategies, so they're stuck.

The fix: Choose the model that actually fits how you want to work, not just what seems "normal" in your field.

Build the Business You Want (Unless You Enjoy Crying in the Shower)

I have built two types of businesses. One that made me want to throw my laptop into the sea and live out my days selling handmade seashell necklaces on the beach… and one that actually felt good to run.

Guess which one I recommend?

See, if you don't get intentional about your business, you'll wake up one day drowning in clients you don't like, stuck in a schedule that exhausts you, and wondering why *you*—the boss—have less freedom than when you worked a 9-to-5.

It sneaks up on you. You say yes to one thing, then another, and before you know it, you're running a business that looks nothing like the life you really want. More stress, less time, and somehow you're working harder than ever just to keep up.

The 3x10 Approach forces you to **pause** and get clear before you end up in that mess. Because let me tell you—building a business that fits **you** is a heck of a lot better than building one that runs you into the ground.

So, take a minute. Picture the *actual* life you want. The business that supports it. Then build *that*.

Otherwise, you might just find yourself barefoot on the side of the road, pricing out seashell necklaces, and pretending it was the plan all along.

Building the business I love allowed me to buy the house near the beach, fly friends in for vacay, build a crazy goldendoodle doggy pack, have the Downton-Abbey house staff "tropical version", and pay for the medical staff needed to live this life, even though I have an incurable primary immune deficiency.

Setting up my life this way has meant the difference between me staying in the game of business vs staying out.

And that has meant being able to have big impact with my clients.

My dream doesn't need to be your dream. But **you need** to choose the right 3x10 Approach to be able to realize your dream.

ACTION STEPS: Identifying Your Ideal Practice Model

- **Choose your practice level.** Are you an Operator, Manager, or Founder? Where are you now and where do you want to go?

- **Pick your business model.** Which of the 10 models excites you most? Try to pick one and stick with it – it is more complicated to jump models.

- **Reality check.** If you build this, will you love your work in five years?

Once you lock this in, everything else becomes easier—your pricing, marketing, hiring, and growth strategy will all align.

Next Up: The Rx5 Formula: The 5 Pillars of a Successful Practice

We'll cover:

Why most businesses fail (and how to make sure yours doesn't).

The 5 Pillars of a thriving practice—Lead Generation, Sales & Offers, Backend & Admin, Clinical Care, and Leadership.

How to identify YOUR weak spots—so you can strengthen them before they hold you back.

Chapter 4 will give you **a bird's-eye view of what it takes to build a practice that lasts**—so you can stop **putting out fires** and start **building something sustainable.**

PS – spend some time on this chapter, for real! Make sure you are building the business you want because it is so common not to. And I'm not saying you have to do an ayahuasca ceremony in the jungle, just take a bath and really think about what you want your typical day to look like?

Chapter 4 - The Rx5 Formula

Why Most Businesses Fail (And How You Won't)

Let's get straight to it—most private practices fail not because of a lack of passion or clinical skills but because **business strategy was never part of the training**.

You can be the most brilliant healer in the world, but if:

- No one knows you exist
- You don't have a system for bringing in and retaining patients
- Your backend is a chaotic mess
- Your leadership is nonexistent…

Then your practice is a campfire in a thunderstorm.

This is **why so many incredible practitioners burn out or struggle financially**. They assume that if they're great at patient care, the business side will magically work itself out.

That's **not** how it works.

A thriving practice isn't built on **one** thing—it's built on **five**.

That's where the **Rx5 Formula** comes in.

Lead Generation	Sales & Offer	Backend & Admin	Clinical Care	Leadership & Mgmt

The 5 Pillars of a Thriving Practice

If you're missing even **one** of these, your business will feel like it's constantly on shaky ground. When you master all **five**, your practice becomes profitable, predictable, and scalable.

Let's break them down.

1. Lead Generation (Marketing) – Getting Patients in the Door

This is the **number one reason practices fail**—they don't have a reliable way to bring in new patients. (Most of this book will be about this Pillar #1).

Marketing is **not optional**. You either attract new patients, or you don't have a business.

The mistake most practitioners make? They rely on:

- Word-of-mouth (great, but not enough).
- Random social media posts (likes won't pay the bills).
- Hoping people "just find them" (hope is not a strategy).

A successful practice has **a system for attracting and converting patients consistently**.

What this means in real life:

- **Know your ideal patient.** You can't market to everyone. Who are you **really** speaking to?

- **Use the right marketing approach.** Pain point marketing, aspirational marketing, promotions, or contrarian messaging—one will resonate best.

- **Understand the marketing funnel.** People don't just "book appointments" out of nowhere. They need to trust you first.

- **Market for where people are.** Hot leads, warm leads, and cold leads all require different strategies.

A practice without **intentional marketing** is a practice that struggles to grow.

2. Sales & Offer – Turning Interest into Revenue

Marketing gets attention. **Sales converts attention into revenue.** (We will cover Pillar #2 briefly in this book).

If you don't know how to **sell your services**, all the marketing in the world won't save you.

The biggest myths practitioners believe:

- "I don't want to be salesy." (Great, don't be. Be **helpful** instead.)

- "If they need me, they'll book." (**Wrong**. People hesitate, procrastinate, and second-guess everything.)

- "I'll just let my prices speak for themselves." (**They won't.**)

A strong sales process means:

- **You confidently present your offer.** Patients need to understand what they're paying for and why.

- **You eliminate friction.** If the booking process is confusing, people won't follow through.

- **You don't undervalue yourself.** If you charge too little, you'll work yourself into exhaustion.

Marketing gets patients **interested**—but if your offer isn't clear or your pricing is weak, they won't commit.

3. Backend & Admin – The Systems That Keep You Sane

This is **where most practitioners hit their breaking point**.

Without the right systems, your practice will **own you** instead of the other way around.

The common problems?

- You feel **overwhelmed** by admin work.
- Your schedule is a **disaster**.
- You're constantly **fixing problems instead of growing**.

The fix:

- **Time management & scheduling.** Your business should run on a **predictable** schedule—not chaos.

- **Automate everything possible.** Patient follow-ups, billing, email sequences—use systems, not your brainpower. Try not to rethink anything you don't have to.

- **Build workflows.** Every repeated task should have a **clear process** to follow.

- **Track financials.** If you don't know your numbers, you're flying blind.

Without systems, you'll feel like you're drowning. **With them, you can finally breathe.**

This pillar never sounds sexy – but it is the long-term work of any business and where freedom comes from. Want to take a month off worry free? Only if you have Backend & Admin (your operations) dialed in!

4. Clinical Care – Delivering Results at Scale

Yes, clinical care is the heart of your business—but how you **deliver** it matters.

Most practitioners **don't have a structured system for patient care**—which means:

- They **reinvent the wheel** with every patient.

- They have **inconsistent results**.

- They get **burned out** because every new patient means starting over and it is exhausting.

A thriving practice has:

- **Clear patient workflows.** Every patient follows a predictable **journey** from consult to results. (This does not mean protocol care; you can still deliver personalized & individualized health and wellness).

- **Efficient intake & onboarding.** The first impression matters—make it smooth and welcoming.

- **Scalable care plans.** You need systems to grow or hire others. Have **frameworks** that guide treatment.

- **Team support.** A good health coach, nurse, or admin can handle **so much** of the work you shouldn't be doing. (Yes, even if you ARE the nurse or the health coach – you are the **CEO** of your business.)

Great patient outcomes happen **when your clinical processes are dialed in**.

PRO TIP: Master the health coaching whether you do it or have someone else deliver it. The hardest part is getting the patient to make the lifestyle changes and "do the thing" and it is the most important part of the job if you want to see real transformations.

5. Leadership & Management – Becoming the CEO of Your Practice

The final pillar—and the **hardest** for most practitioners—is **stepping into leadership**.

If your business **relies on you for everything**, you **don't** own a business. You own a job.

Leadership means:

- **You hire the right team**—so you don't do everything yourself.

- **You make decisions quickly**—instead of getting stuck in overthinking.

- **You focus on growth**—not just patient care.

Your business can **only** grow as far as your leadership allows. (Make sure you have clear directions for your team).

Why Mastering All 5 is Critical

Here's the **painful truth**:

Most practices **only focus on 1 or 2 pillars**—and that's why they hit ceilings.

- If you only focus on clinical care but ignore marketing, **you'll struggle to get patients.**

- If you only focus on marketing but ignore backend systems, **you'll drown in admin work.**

- If you only focus on patient acquisition but ignore sales, **you'll attract people who never commit.**

Your practice isn't **just a clinic**—it's a **business.**

You don't need to be **perfect** at all five pillars, but you **do** need to make sure none of them are ignored.

ACTION STEPS: Evaluating Your Strength in Each Pillar

- **Rate yourself from 1-10 on each of the 5 pillars.** Be honest—where are you thriving, and where are you struggling?
- **Identify your biggest weak spot.** What's the **one** thing causing the most stress in your business?
- **Commit to improving that pillar first.** You don't have to fix everything at once—just focus on **one** major area at a time.

Next up: Why This Book Focuses on Offers Before Marketing

Because I'm trying to torture you – you bought a book on marketing and I'm trying to drive you crazy by not starting the marketing convo until Chapter 8.

I know it might feel that way – but the truth is, getting clear on everything we've talked about so far up to this point plus offers which we are about to cover next (briefly) - will **determine** so much of your marketing.

I just didn't feel good jumping into marketing until you were better set up and that means knowing what the heck you are going to offer.

In Chapter 5 (& 6, & 7), let's make sure you know what you are selling before we try to plan the marketing for it!

PS – Don't skip these next chapters, sister! I know you want to. I know you are chomping at the bit - "Give me the marketing already, damn it!"

Please hear me – it is with love and a cattle prod that I tell you that you need these next few chapters. Read them. **Do the work.**

Chapter 5 - Marketing Pause - Get Ready to Talk Offers

If You Don't Know What You're Selling, How Do You Market It?

Let's play a quick game.

Imagine you open an online store, but you're not really sure what you're selling yet. Maybe socks? Maybe fancy notebooks? Maybe hand-knit sweaters for emotional support hamsters?

Now, try running ads. Try writing social media posts. Try telling people why they should buy from you.

Feels impossible, right?

That's what happens when you try to market your practice without first knowing exactly what you're offering.

Marketing (Pillar 1 – Lead Generation) is all about **getting people's attention** and **attracting potential patients.** But if you don't know what you're leading them to… then you're just making a lot of *noise* with no clear destination.

So, while this book is **focused on marketing**, we need to have a little fun detour into **Pillar 2 (Sales & Offer),** because the two are **inseparable.**

Marketing brings people in the door.

Your offer (Pillar 2) is what convinces them to stay.

Let's break this down before we dive headfirst into marketing strategies—because trust me, it'll make everything smoother from here on out.

Why Lead Generation (Pillar 1) Is the #1 Thing That Determines Success

If your practice were a car, **marketing would be the engine.**

You could have the most beautifully designed car in the world, the comfiest seats, and a premium sound system, but **if there's no engine, it's not going anywhere.**

This is where a lot of practitioners get stuck. They focus on:

- Getting more certifications
- Perfecting their systems
- Creating the "ultimate" patient experience
- Buying fancy equipment

But if they don't have a **steady flow of new patients coming in,** none of that stuff matters.

Marketing is what **keeps your practice moving forward.**

Wait… But What If I'm Not Sure What I'm Selling Yet?

Ah, excellent question.

Because **THIS is why we need to do a quick stop in Pillar 2 (Sales & Offer) before going any deeper into marketing.**

Here's the thing:

- You **can't** run ads if you don't know what you're advertising.

- You **can't** write a great website if you don't know what you're trying to sell.

- You **can't** generate leads if you don't know what happens AFTER they become a lead.

Most practitioners get stuck in marketing because they haven't fully nailed down their offer.

So, before we talk about "getting more patients," we need to **make sure you know exactly what you're leading them toward.**

What This Book Covers (And What It Doesn't)

This book is about **Mastering Pillar 1 (Marketing & Lead Generation).**

By the time we're done, you'll know how to:

- **Get in front of the right people** instead of shouting into the void.

- **Attract patients who actually want what you offer.**

- **Stop relying on word-of-mouth as your only strategy.**

- **Turn marketing into a system**—so you're not constantly wondering where your next patient is coming from.

What This Book Does Not Cover (But We'll Touch on a Little Anyway)

- **Pillar 2: Sales & Offer** – You must know what you're selling before you can market it. That's why **next chapter, we're going to play around with Pillar 2 just enough to get you unstuck.**

- **Pillar 3: Backend & Admin** – If you're running around like a headless chicken trying to keep your practice organized, that's an admin problem, not a marketing problem. Future books will tackle this.

- **Pillar 4: Clinical Care** – I'm assuming you're already a great practitioner. If you're not, no amount of marketing will fix that. Take our certifications, we'll get you up to speed in no time and feeling clinically confident to boot! See the Additional Resources for our Clinical Core Monthly – we've got this solved!

- **Pillar 5: Leadership & Management** – Eventually, you'll want to stop doing everything yourself and build a team. But that's a later problem. First, let's make sure your **marketing** is working.

The Role of Pillar 2 (Sales & Offer) in Marketing Success

Let's be real. You don't just want **any** patients. You want the **right** patients. The ones who actually value what you do, are ready to commit, and don't treat you like a human WebMD search bar.

But **attracting the right people requires knowing exactly what you're offering them.**

That's why before we go full speed into marketing, next chapter we're going to **take a moment to refine your offer.**

It won't be overwhelming. It won't be complicated. But I promise **it will make marketing 100x easier.**

You Can't Sell a Mystery (Unless You're in the Business of Psychic Readings)

Look, I've tried to "wing it" before. Launched offers without really knowing what I was selling, figured I'd just explain it when people asked, and hoped the details would magically sort themselves out.

Spoiler alert: That did not work.

Turns out, people don't want vague. They don't want, *"Well, it's kind of a wellness program, but also kind of a coaching package, and sometimes I throw in lab testing, and, you know, we'll see what happens."* No. They want clarity. They want to know, *"What am I getting? How does it work? Will this solve my problem?"*

And if you don't know the answers, your potential patients sure as heck won't either.

This is why you cannot—***cannot***—skip dialing in your offer. Otherwise, your marketing will feel like shouting into the void, hoping someone, somewhere, will just *figure it out* and hand over their credit card.

Spoiler alert #2: That also does not work.

Nothing is worse than building a marketing machine… only to realize you've built it around something that makes you want to fake a Wi-Fi outage whenever a sales call pops up.

ACTION STEPS: Get Ready for Some Offer Tweaking

- **Think about your current offer.** Do you have **one** clear, compelling way that people work with you, or is it a vague "schedule a consult" free-for-all?

- **Write down the exact transformation you provide.** What do your patients get by working with you? Be specific.

- **Be honest—do you love your offer?** If marketing feels like pushing a boulder up a hill, it might be time for some adjustments.

Next Up: Let's Make Sure You're Selling the Right Thing

Marketing is **so much easier** when you love what you're selling.

So, before we dive into lead generation, which is the rest of this book, next chapter, we're going to make sure your offer is clear, compelling, and **aligned with what you actually want to build.**

Trust me, Chapter 6 will make everything flow better. Let's go.

Chapter 6 - Creating an Irresistible Offer

Why Great Marketing Can't Fix a Bad Offer

Marketing is **not** a magic trick. If your **offer** is weak, confusing, or just plain unappealing, **no amount of marketing will save it.**

You could have:

The best ads.

The best branding.

The best website.

And you'd **still** hear crickets if your offer isn't **crystal clear and compelling.**

This is where so many practitioners struggle. They think they have an offer when, really, they just have a **list of services.**

"I do functional medicine."

"I offer chiropractic care."

"I help people get healthier."

That's not an offer. That's a profession.

A **great offer** answers four essential questions:

- **What problem are you solving?**
- **How do you solve it?**
- **Why should someone choose YOU?**
- **How easy is it to say yes?**

If your offer isn't **specific, simple, and irresistible**, marketing will feel like pushing a boulder uphill—**while wearing roller skates and dodging flying debris.**

How to Create an Offer That Sells Itself

Your offer should be **so compelling** that when your ideal patient hears about it, they instantly think, **"YES, I need this."**

Step 1: Define the Before & After

People **don't really pay for functional medicine or integrative care or alternative medicine.** They pay for **transformation** (or answers, or results, or to understand).

Here's what they actually care about:

- **Before:** I'm exhausted all the time.
- **After:** I finally have energy again.
- **Before:** I can't lose weight no matter what I try.
- **After:** I feel confident and strong in my body.
- **Before:** I have constant bloating and digestive issues.

- **After:** I can eat without pain and discomfort.

You are selling **a transformation,** not just a service.

Here are **real-life examples** of what people want:

- I'm overweight and I want to be thin.
- I yell at my kids, and I want to be a calm mom.
- I'm up all night and I really want to sleep.
- I can't stop eating Taco Bell and I want to start eating like an adult.
- My dad died from a heart attack, and I want to avoid getting one.
- I'm constantly bloated and just want to eat without feeling like I swallowed a balloon.

We call this going from "misery island" to "paradise island" and no one cares about the bridge that gets you there – they just want off misery island!

Full disclosure – there is a spot to talk about the "bridge" and that is when you get into your unique mechanism (aka point of view, unique selling proposition) and you can share some of your "how" there. But as practitioners, most of you talk this up to death *so reel it back.*

Your job is to **paint a clear before-and-after picture** that makes the transformation obvious.

Step 2: Make It New, Easy, and Different

People are wired to believe in things that are **new and different**—it gives them **hope.**

Your offer needs to highlight:

- **A new approach** (something they haven't tried before).

- **An easy process** (clear, step-by-step, no confusion).

- **A superior solution** (why this works better than anything else).

For example:

Weak Offer: "I help people lose weight with functional medicine."

Strong Offer: "The Weight Reset Program: A science-backed, doctor-led program that fixes your metabolism so you can lose weight and keep it off—without restrictive dieting or insane workouts."

People believe in "new" and "different" because it provides **hope.** So, figure out what's new and different about **you**, your **approach**, your **technique**, or your **method.**

- A **meal plan** that will have your **skin glowing within days.**

- A **superior form of bodywork** using **movement science blended with ancient yoga.**

- The **answer to sleepless nights** that's **pill-free, government-backed, and newly available.**

- **The easiest way to stop sugar cravings—fast!**

Rule #1: Always tell the **truth**. Make sure you can **back up your claims** and follow all **legal guidelines**.

Step 3: Choose the Right Offer Format

People buy in three ways:

- **Done for You (Premium $$$)** – Concierge health services, meal delivery, high-end testing.
- **Done with You (Mid-Range $$)** – Programs with coaching, guided step-by-step plans.
- **Do It Yourself (Low-Cost $)** – Digital courses, books, meal plans.

The easier and more convenient you make it; the more people will pay for it.

PRO TIP: The best offers include all 3!

Step 4: It Has to Be Worth It!

Keep in mind, **Functional Medicine and lifestyle interventions can be HARD** because it *requires* patient participation.

For someone to commit, the transformation needs to be worth the effort.

Massive consequence of staying the same (what's at stake if they don't change?).

Big desirable result (what's the clear benefit?).

The juice must be worth the squeeze.

Examples:

- **Willing to take vitamin D** if it helps prevent cardiovascular disease.

- **Willing to do an elimination diet** if it stops unbearable itching.

- **Willing to follow your meal plan** if it finally gets the weight off.

- **Willing to do vagal tone exercises** if it stops stress-induced meltdowns.

Step 5: The Key Point – Make Your Offer Stand Out

Every great offer has a Key Point – this has been taught in sales for decades – don't miss it!

Your Key Point should include:

Clear Benefits – Tangible, measurable results.

Emotionally Compelling Connections– What the patient truly wants.

Intellectual or **Organization** Systems– A unique, science-backed, fascinating angle.

Unique Mechanism (UM aka POV aka USP) – Your specific or special method or approach.

Example:

- **Before/After:** Overweight → Thin.

- **Clear Benefit:** Lose weight, fit into jeans.

- **Emotionally Compelling:** Feel attractive, confident, energetic.

- **Intellectually Interesting:** Combining hormonal science with ancient medicine.

- **Unique Mechanism: The Hormone 5E Reset Program – Ends Sugar Cravings in 3 Days.**

If **other providers offer similar services**, your **Unique Mechanism** is what sets you apart.

Planning Your Offer: Like a Dental Procedure, but Worth It

I once spent six weeks—*six full weeks*—agonizing over an offer. I questioned everything. Was it too simple? Too complicated? Too expensive? Too cheap? Should I add another bonus? What about a new name? Should I just scrap it and move to the woods?

At times, it felt like trying to write a dissertation while a toddler repeatedly asked, *"But why?"* in the background.

But here's the thing: That offer became one of my biggest successes. Because all that work—the painful overthinking, the tweaking, the *oh-my-god-why-am-I-still-doing-this* moments—paid off.

And that's what I want you to remember when your brain starts spiraling into *I should just wing it* territory.

A clear, intentional offer is the foundation of everything else. It's what makes marketing easy, pricing confident, and sales *not* feel like an awkward high-pressure pitch.

So, take the time now. Yes, it might make you want to scream into a pillow. But future-you—the one who isn't scrambling to explain what they do every time someone asks—will be *very* grateful.

ACTION STEPS: Build Your Irresistible Offer

Write down your **current offer. Is it clear, simple, and compelling?**

Your offer should make sense for the 3x10 Approach (level and model) that you chose.

If you're in The Dr Z Functional Medicine Academy we have "done-for-you" examples and a very detailed system to help you build a tight offer – do it!

Make sure you have **ONE clear offer.**

Next Up: Pricing, Money Myths & Buyer's Ease

Now that you've built an irresistible offer, it's time to price it correctly and overcome money mindset blocks.

In Chapter 7, we're tackling **pricing, eliminating limiting beliefs**, and making it easy for **patients to say YES**.

Let's go!

PS – **Yes**, we're getting closer to the "real marketing" parts. We're almost there. You have to deal with pricing and money though, otherwise forget marketing because all marketing (should) lead to sales which involves money.

Yes, there will be a money exchange. This is a good thing, not a bad thing. Read the next chapter, I've got you.

Afterwards, once you've gotten through the whole book and you are now a different person, a different business owner, capable of eating stress for breakfast and spitting out Benjamins for dessert...

You might want to send me dark chocolate tower gift baskets as a thank you.

Too soon? No worries. I'll wait.

Chapter 7 - The Money Mindset & Pricing Strategy

Why Your Pricing & Mindset Determine Your Success

Let's talk about money—the thing nobody wants to talk about, but everybody stresses over.

You can have the best offer, but if your pricing is off or your money mindset is sabotaging you, you're going to *struggle*.

Many practitioners:

- Feel guilty charging what they're worth
- Assume patients can't afford their services
- Think wealthy people are bad and don't want to become one of them
- Worry that raising prices will scare people away

Here's the problem: If **you** aren't confident about your pricing, your patients won't be either.

This chapter is here to help you fix that, so you can get paid what you deserve, serve more people, and finally stop stressing about money.

Step 1: Price Your Offer Correctly

A weak offer can become strong just by adjusting the price and positioning.

The simple rule:

The bigger the transformation, the higher the price.

Think about it: People pay

- $5 for a coffee because it's convenient, fast, and feels premium
- $3,000 for a mattress because they value a good night's sleep
- $10,000 for a surgery because it changes their life

But most practitioners undercharge. Why?

Because they're pricing based on their own fears instead of the true value of their work.

Three Ways to Price Your Offer:

- **Done-for-You (Premium)** – Concierge health services, meal delivery, high-end testing
- **Done-with-You (Mid-Range)** – Programs with coaching, guided step-by-step plans
- **Do-It-Yourself (Low-Cost)** – Digital courses, books, meal plans

Your pricing should reflect:

- The transformation you provide
- The level of service and support
- The *value* of the problem you solve

Step 2: The Buyer's Ease Formula – Make It an Easy "Yes"

Ever notice how some things are just easy to buy?

- Amazon one-click checkout
- Uber—tap, ride, done
- Netflix—subscribe, watch forever

Good business offers ***remove friction*** so that saying yes feels **effortless**.

Your offer (whether delivered in-person, online, or via presentations) should include most (if not all) of **The Buyer's Ease Formula.**

Create Buyer's Ease

Create an Irresistible Offer that becomes an easy yes!

Even the best marketing can't make up for a bad offer AND a great offer is so important!!!!

- NAME - have a descriptive name of the "thing" that you are selling
- TRANSFORMATION - that is clear and undeniable!
- JUSTIFICATION - What special, new, intro, or the reason its available now?
- CONSEQUENCES - of staying the same, no change
- BIG WIN - what happens when you make the decision
- BENEFITS - for each feature - "what's in it for me?", make it felt & seen
- PRICING - give us much value as you can
- PAYMENT - are there pay options, flexibility
- GUARANTEE - Risk reversal
- LIMITER - scarcity, limited space, deadline, price change, why act now?
- BONUS - Incentive - premium - special bundle - for first X

- **Name** – Have a clear, descriptive name for what you are offering

- **Transformation** – The change they will experience should be clear and undeniable

- **Justification** – What's special, new, or unique? Why is it available now?

- **Consequences** – What happens if they stay the same and don't take action?

- **Big Win** – What happens when they say yes? What's the ultimate payoff?

- **Benefits** – For each feature, answer: "What's in it for me?" (from the patient's perspective)

- **Pricing** – Make it obvious why it's worth it

- **Payment Options** – Flexible payment plans make it easier to say yes

- **Guarantee** – Offer risk reversal. How do you make this a safe decision?

- **Limiter** – Scarcity, deadline, or limited spots—why should they act now?

- **Bonus** – Extra incentive for fast action

The goal is to make your offer so good, so clear, and so valuable that saying yes is effortless, obvious, a no-brainer, and doesn't require you to be "salesy".

Step 3: Work through the 5 Money Myths that keep Practitioners Stuck

Your offer is *only* as good as your mindset around money.

Most practitioners struggle to charge their worth because of deeply ingrained beliefs about money. I understand, I **had** to work through this myself.

Some lessons I learned the hard way. And then, if I didn't fully get it - life threw me more curveballs until I finally got it.

Not having enough money is hard, stressful, and can feel very heavy.

There is a huge range of things that contribute to money issues and this section of the book won't cover all of them.

This section will talk about some of the childhood messaging or programming, society expectations, self-sabotage, and really just **YOUR** personal relationship with money.

It's an important relationship to consider for all of us, but **absolutely essential** if you are going to own your own business.

I will mostly share from my experiences and perspective that I have lived with the hope that it will help you with your unique money journey.

MYTH #1. "I Don't Care About Money."

This is one I embraced for a long time. I'm an idealist, I'm creative, I'm a nurturer and healer - money is beneath me.

This led to me being *uninformed, overspending, under-earning, under-charging, not holding good boundaries, being taken advantage* of… just a host of problems for decades!

Saying I didn't care about money was like saying I didn't care if we had shelter or food. It's just **a basic tool** in our society for survival and I was hurting myself by not fully understanding it.

I didn't want to be crass or tacky so I wouldn't talk about money - but we **lose our power** when we keep secrets or won't face something head on.

I didn't want to seem greedy, so I undercharged - and that made it hard to operate in business and then very money focused all the time (**opposite** of what I wanted) because of stress.

I didn't want to seem like money mattered more than people (and it doesn't) so I wouldn't enforce appointment cancellation policies or had a difficult time establishing boundaries - but that led to people taking advantage and feelings of resentment.

MYTH #2. "I Only Need to Make a Little Money."

Another favorite mantra of those suffering from insecurity or a lack of worth or playing the martyr role - and I was stuck in it for years!

Do you know what making *"just a little"* money feels like?

It constantly feels like **one foot away from nothing at all**. It's like someone who is hungry, and you give them one bite of an apple a day. All you can think about is food, how hungry you are, and how you don't have enough.

I thought I was being generous by only needing an "itty bitty" profit but that completely backfired.

Instead, I had to say "no" to a lot of things including giving a discount for a patient (I couldn't afford it), hiring new staff or giving raises, taking time off, activities with my family, donating to charity, donating my time - it was the **exact opposite of a generous state**.

I completely underestimated the impact of constant money stress until I was on the other side of this and earning a decent profit. When that stress was gone, I was able to truly show up in a generous and energized way. It was **remarkable**.

3. "Wealthy People Are Bad."

Some are, no doubt - but this is a dangerous myth to stereotype a group in this way. In my personal experience, good people who make more money then do more good things.

I can't wait to be so wealthy that I can run around like a fairy godmother and do endless good deeds. How much fun would that be?!? Sounds delightful.

Characterizing wealthy people as bad also creates an **"us vs them"** mentality and is a great way to stay on the poverty side because you don't belong or can't relate to those that have money.

Well, carve your own way honey!

Start creating new stereotypes about what happens when someone like you makes great money…and all the great things you'll do.

4. "I Just Can't Imagine Earning $XYZ."

This has held me back a lot - just a lack of imagination and experience with $XYZ dollar amount so then it doesn't seem real or attainable.

It definitely contributed to me hitting my own glass ceiling.

Three different times I made the same amount the first year in business in three different industries. **Hmmm...that's odd.**

I managed to make each business profitable, and it was multiple 6-figures so it wasn't like I was slacking - but I was limited by what I thought was **reasonable**.

Finally, I decided to break past that and have a bigger vision. And I believed I could do it faster and I got the coaching help to provide the guidance...And then I did it.

I look back now and just sigh. I made it so hard for myself in the past and I didn't need to. I just needed a bigger vision.

5. "Making Money Is Too Hard."

Another favorite self-sabotage of mine that I've recycled over the years.

I've used this as an excuse for why I can not accomplish something and loved to tie it into my health challenges, or relationships, or parenting, or whatever flavor of the month had me say - *"I just can't do this - I'm not capable - I don't belong".*

Sometimes I throw in *"I'm too fat"*, *"I'm too old"*, and *"I'm not a dude"* just for good measure - when I *really* want to guarantee failure.

And then I will search for evidence (and when you search, you always find it) of how it's **not** working, how people are disappointing me and I can't count on anyone, how it was a dumb idea and I'm going to break...

When really all I need is a **nap and a plan**.

Can't I just go back in time and take all the knowledge and wisdom I have at 50 and give it to my 20-year-old self? Please?!?

I HAVE LIVED ALL 5 OF THESE THINGS ABOVE.

I have earned money and at one point owned 8 homes. I have also been broke and on social security disability. I have had to restart and reinvent after a major life challenge. I have earned a lot of money all at one time and I've donated a lot of money. I've had long periods of time where I lived on a tight budget and said no to every extra. I used to hate sales with such a passion that I wouldn't say the word and was proud of my poverty mentality, like it was a badge of honor.

What I know is that **actual money** had very little to do with those things, that it was mostly just all me, where I was in my growth and what I believed was possible.

At this point in my life, I love to talk about money as much as I love to talk about poop and digestion and hormones and parenting and traveling...I'm not afraid of it anymore, it no longer has power over me.

Which leads me to a secret that I absolutely must share with you.

The **BEST** way to get out of debt, provide for your family, fund that dream is...

SECRET #1 - TO MAKE MORE MONEY!!!

For real!

You can *not* save your way out of debt. You cannot budget your way to becoming wealthy. You cannot find just the right job that will end your financial woes.

I've tried them all and by far the best was to just make more money.

And that leads me to another secret.

SECRET #2 - YOU ARE YOUR BEST INVESTMENT - HANDS DOWN.

I've tried everything else - stocks, bonds, mutual funds, managed accounts, index accounts, AI investing, property lien bonds, crypto, real estate and more…and there is a place for them in your life.

But **nothing** pays out like you putting in the work to build a profitable business.

Nothing gives you the leverage and large cash windfall that a successful launch or profitable business can **generate** - while also giving you more control over the input and the output.

You can basically **be your own bank.**

IF you are willing to do the work.

Once I got past the money modes of too little, just enough, working hard not to lose it and to a place of being able to breathe and really relax and not feeling so stressed - well, then **I wanted that for everyone!!!**

To get there, you have to release the 5 myths above and embrace the 2 secrets.

Let me add one last tip - yet another gift of turning 50+.

Tip - **RUN at life!**

Really, run at life and live a day fully so that you've participated and go to bed actually tired.

No one has time for doom-scrolling when they've lived a day fully.

Run at life and take big leaps toward your goals. Live like this is the only life you get - because it's not a dress rehearsal. We don't know what's on the other side, but you do know what is here now - so make the most of it.

Run at life because we don't know how much time we've got (sorry for sounding morose, but it's true!) and there is **NO TIME** to delay your dreams.

Following that advice has led me to many places over the last few years from moving to another country, hiring superstars, investing in myself, launching a business, and much more.

I regret exactly ZERO of it.

Not everything is a win and not every day is a party - but we tend to regret the things we don't do, not the swings at life.

So don't hesitate - run at life!

Step 4: Questions to Ask Yourself

If you struggle with pricing, money, or making your offer more attractive, ask yourself:

- Why should someone choose you?

- Why is your solution unique or different?

- What's the transformation you're promising?

- Are you pricing based on fear or value?

- Are you making it easy for people to say yes?

- Do you believe in the value of your work?

- Are you making assumptions about what people can afford?

- What are your own limiting beliefs about money?

- Have you positioned your pricing in a way that makes sense to your ideal patient?

- Do you need to raise your prices to reflect your true value?

If you can't answer these confidently, refine your offer before moving forward.

ACTION STEPS: Money & Pricing

- Review your pricing. Does it reflect the **value** of the transformation you provide?

- Run your offer through The Buyer's Ease Formula.

- Check your money mindset. Are you holding onto any limiting beliefs?

- Ask yourself: "Why wouldn't I buy this?" Fix any objections.

- Make sure you have ONE clear offer. Packages, or programs, plus recurring memberships work best.

Next Up: Finding Your Ideal Patient

We're going to dive into:

Character Codes – How to identify and adapt to different patient personalities for better communication and higher conversions.

Patient Interviews – How to conduct interviews that uncover exactly what your patients are struggling with (so your marketing writes itself).

Real-Life Messaging – How to craft outreach and content that instantly resonates with your audience.

Because when you **speak their language**, your marketing becomes effortless—and your ideal patients start coming to you.

Chapter 8, let's get into it!

PS – This is it!!! The real marketing section – finally!!! Sigh. Whew. Relief. OMG, I'll have what she's having moment...Let's go!

Chapter 8 - Choosing Your Ideal Patient

How to Attract, Connect, and Serve Your People—Without the Headaches

Let's be honest—some patients are a dream to work with. They follow the plan, respect your time, and send referrals. Others... not so much.

The difference between a **thriving** practice and a **burnt-out** practitioner?

Knowing exactly who you serve best.

If you don't define your ideal patient, you'll end up:

- Attracting people who aren't a good fit.

- Struggling to convert leads because your messaging is too vague.

- Wasting time on patients who drain your energy instead of fueling your mission.

And the worst part? **You start questioning if it's even worth it.**

That's why we use the 3-Step Ideal Patient Formula - a simple framework to help you find and connect with the right people effortlessly.

3-Step
Ideal Patient Formula

1. Demographics
Basic start (can be helpful with ad targeting) to include gender, age, and often location.

2. Niche
We are talking marketing so yes - you want to pick a niche which could be a focus on a symptom, condition, issue, complaint, group of people...lots of options!

3. Character Code
No ideal patient formula is complete without it - choose your Character Code and USE those marketing identities - it makes all the difference!

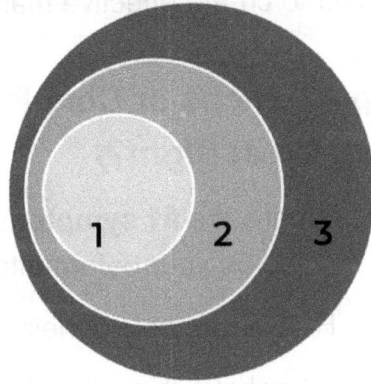

1: The 3-Step Ideal Patient Formula

The typical advice says, *"Create an avatar! What's their name? Where do they shop? What do they eat for breakfast?"*

That's cute. But not helpful.

Here's the **real** way to define your ideal patient—using 3 key elements:

Step #1. Demographics

- Age, gender, location
- Occupation, income level
- Marital/family status, or specific population/group (optional)
- Where they spend time online (optional)

Example: Women with kids in their 40s–50s in Tennessee

Great, now we have a starting point. But this alone **isn't enough** to create effective marketing.

Step #2. Niche or Core Problem *(What's Keeping Them Up at Night?)*

- What's the **#1 symptom** they're struggling with? This could be your before/after.

- How is it affecting their life?

- What have they tried that didn't work?

- Why haven't they solved this yet?

- If not marketing for a symptom or condition, is it how they've experienced traditional healthcare? Or a key complaint, issue, need to be heard, or looking for answers?

Examples:

By Before/After:

- Fat to Thin.

- Acne to Clear Skin.

By condition:

- PCOS or Fibromyalgia or SIBO or Diabetes .

- Be mindful of regulations for your licensing regarding marketing for diagnosable conditions (see Chapter 19).

By issue/complaint:

- "They're exhausted, gaining weight, and irritable. Their doctor says their labs are 'normal,' but they feel anything but. They've tried diets, hormone creams, and random supplements—nothing works."

By need to be heard:

- "I'm tired of being told it's 'In my head', won't anyone take me seriously?"

Step #3. The Character Code System™ – How they think, act, and buy – so you can speak their language!

Most ideal client/patient marketing fails because they **don't** account for personality types.

The truth: If you talk to *every* patient the same way, you'll lose them.

People make decisions **differently** based on their dominant personality traits.

CHARACTER
CODE INTRO

Class President

Cheerleader

Actor

Tasks   People   Both

Scholar

Activist

Artist

The Character Code System™ helps you quickly identify these traits so you can market to a specific ideal patient and then adjust your approach for communication, so your message is heard and understood.

Important Note: The power of these techniques lies in intention. **Use them ethically, with integrity, and always in service of helping others.** True impact comes from aligning skill with purpose – let your work be a **force for good.**

Here is a very brief, basic sample below. Grab the handouts and watch the video training for full details – it's important! (See Additional Resources in the back.)

Basic Character Code Example
(Grab Handouts for Essential Details!)

Character Code	How They Think	Marketing Example
Class President	Confident, decisive, likes control.	"The fastest way to fix this problem. No fluff—just results."
Cheerleader	Social, fun-loving, thrives on excitement.	"Join a community of women healing their hormones together!"
Actor	Expressive, emotional, loves drama.	"You're NOT crazy. Let's kick 'hormonal chaos' to the curb!"

Basic Character Code Example
(Grab Handouts for Essential Details!)

Character Code	How They Think	Marketing Example
Activist	Heartfelt, passionate, values connection.	"Tired of doctors rushing you and not taking the time to listen? I'm here."
Artist	Unique, independent, doesn't like uniformity.	"No cookie-cutter plans. Your body, your unique journey."
Scholar	Logical, data-driven, needs proof.	"Proven, evidence-based program backed by science."

Why This Works:

If you're marketing to a **Scholar** and hit them with, "You deserve to be heard and loved," they'll roll their eyes and leave. They want **data, facts, and evidence.**

If you're talking to a **Cheerleader** and start quoting PubMed studies, they'll zone out. They want energy, excitement, and **social proof.**

This is where **real** marketing power comes from. Because when you can describe their struggle *better* than they can, **they automatically assume you have the solution – they feel known, seen, and heard.**

I am only *briefly* mentioning Character Codes here, but don't **underestimate the power!**

I created this system about 17 years ago and it has been one of the secrets to my success. My original system was published by McGraw-Hill, NY ("How to Read a Client From Across the Room").

You can watch a quick video of me teaching this and grab our detailed handout with all the information and even take the Character Code Quiz.

NOTE: You aren't using the 3-Step Ideal Patient Formula until you answer and **combine all 3 steps**.

PRO TIP: Get my handout with the Character Code Marketing Identities - an absolute game changer for marketing and my secret behind my $0-$7 million offer! Grab it **HERE** or type

https://get.thedrz.com/idealpatientformula-MMM into your
url browser.

2: How to Conduct Interviews (Without Wasting Time)

The Mistake Most Practitioners Make:

They **assume** they know what potential patients want—without
actually asking.

Bad idea.

The **best** marketing language comes *directly* from people –
real people.

And the easiest way to get it? **Interviews.**

Yes, this is *after* you have identified your ideal patient using
the 3-step formula above.

Next, **you talk to them.**

Think about it, corporations spend millions running focus
groups to test a product and practitioners open up a practice or

launch a program online and have *never* talked to a live, breathing human!

Crazy!!!

Why Interviews Are Game-Changing:

You hear their pain points in **their own words.**

You learn how they think, decide, and talk about their problems.

You get insights you'd NEVER get from a Google search or ChatGPT.

And bonus: **You build relationships that lead to referrals.**

How to Get People to Say YES to an Interview

Let's be honest—people love to talk about their struggles. They just need a good reason.

Here's how you make it **irresistible:**

Make it sound **easy & fun** ("5-minute chat, totally casual!").

Make it about **them**, not you ("I just want to hear your story!").

Example Outreach Messages for Interviews

Example #1:

"Who wants to talk to a doctor for free? Spoiler alert: It's me! I'm looking for women suffering from eczema and adult acne that just won't quit! You've tried the dermatologist, you've bought everything in Sephora, and you have enough bottles of cream to fill a small kiddie pool... I want to talk to you!

If I can borrow just 5 minutes of your time, I would be so grateful! I want to hear what has worked, what doesn't work, what you wish your doctors knew... our discussion will be entirely confidential, free of charge, very short, and help me make sure that my "Smooth Skin" Program is ready to meet the needs of all of my patients. So, they will be thanking you too!

Please comment or message me privately and, again, a big thank you for giving me a few moments of your time. We can chat on the phone or Zoom-- whatever is best for you. And this doctor is ready to listen!"

Example #2:

"Adult-onset acne is awful and I'm determined to do something about it! Please help me and share your stories (100% confidential) as it will help me make sure I'm building the best "Smooth Skin" program for my patients possible!

Please chat with me one-on-one for a few minutes-- I want to hear your complaints, your bad doctor visits, the horrible creams or alternative therapies you tried that didn't work... and any great successes you found that did work!

Please comment or message me privately and I'd love to hear your story!"

Example #3:

"HELP NEEDED-- Please!!!

Fabulous FB family and friends, I'm working with a tyrant business coach, and I must talk to 25 women in the next couple of days-- OMG, please talk to me.

Here's who I'm looking for: any women who feel like they have thyroid issues but their Primary Care Doctor says, "you're fine" and keeps blowing them off.

Totally confidential, I just want to hear your complaints, what you wish your doctors were doing, and research you've done on your own, what has and hasn't worked...

And did I mention-- I must talk to 25 women in just a few days?!

Please help, message me if you can spare 5 minutes of your time, and please SHARE with your friends and on your FB page if possible..."

Example #4:

Adult Acne Sufferers-- I want to hear your complaints! Painful cystic acne around your chin, caustic creams that burn your skin, can't stand looking in the mirror, cancelling dinner plans with friends, scared to date or have a job interview?

Please tell me everything, totally confidential! I want to hear:

What your experience has been

Who helped you-- and who did NOT help you?

What your wish your doctor knew...

Tips you learned the hard way that every acne sufferer should know."

Outreach calls

Besides social media, you can also make outreach calls and ask, "who do you know who might be willing to do a short interview?". Call your:

- Busy-body aunt
- Friends
- Family
- Your neighbors

In-person networking:

Sounds weird, but you can just "go where the people are" and talk to them.

Consider:

- Leaving the house!
- Talking to your neighbors
- Checking the community pool
- Try networking events

What to Say During the Interview:

- "Thank you for your time", tell them how they will be helping you

- Set the agenda, ask for permission
- Ask questions (do NOT make it a health interview, keep in "lay language")
- What are you experiencing? What's bothering you?
- Did you talk to a practitioner about it? How did they treat you?
- Did anything make it better or worse?
- How is this impacting your life?
- How does that make you feel?
- What do you wish your doctor knew about XYZ?
- What do you wish your doctor would have done?
- If you could have a magic wand and it was all better, what would that look like? How would that feel?
- What do you hate about XYZ?
- Is there anything good about XYZ?
- What would life be like if XYZ was totally gone?
- Anything else you want me to know?
- Any questions you have for me?
- Ask for others to talk to - Who else do you know who is also dealing with this that would be willing to chat with me for a few minutes?
- Thank you!

PRO TIP: Write down their exact words. (record it, with permission, if allowed)

If multiple people say, "Menopause makes me feel like I'm on fire," then **use that phrase in your marketing.**

The importance of interviews

- You get out of your shell.

- You learn how to approach people – this is often your first marketing test – did you even get the ideal potential patients for interviews that you were looking for? If you want women with thyroid symptoms but get truckers with hemorrhoids then it's not working. Better to test this while it's free and nothing to sell before we put something really important on the line or do paid advertising!

- You can see how one person connects to another-- you're not trying to sell the people you're talking to on your product, but now that they're aware, they could share that information to someone else!

- You get great marketing language out of it! It helps you make better offers this way.

3: Bringing It All Together: The Ideal Patient Roadmap

Define Your Ideal Patient: (Demographics + Niche + Character Code)

Adjust Your Messaging: Speak their language based on their **Character Code.**

Interview Patients: Borrow their words for your marketing—
it's amazing, I promise.

Finding Your People (So You Don't End Up Serving Everyone and Their Dog)

A practitioner once had a patient inquiry from a guy who—
within five minutes—told her that he "didn't really believe in
functional medicine" but still wanted to "pick her brain" (for
free, of course). Another time, someone asked if she could
cure their chronic migraines… via a single Facebook
comment.

This is what happens when you don't get clear on your ideal
patient. You end up marketing to *everyone*, which means you
attract people who aren't even remotely a good fit. It's like
throwing a backyard all-you-can-eat rib barbecue and realizing
half your guests are vegan, or on an all-cabbage diet.

When I finally nailed down my ideal patient—who they were,
what they struggled with, how they made decisions—
everything changed. My marketing clicked. My sales felt
easier. And best of all? I actually **liked** the people I was
working with.

And why was this book named "Middle-Aged Mama in a
Muumuu"? Because part of your ideal patient formula and
marketing magic is **you being you**. Don't hide you in your
brand, **amplify** it.

It's hard to pretend to be someone else, I really don't
recommend it.

I've taught weight loss challenges and just did them with my patients during phases of my practice where I was feeling a little thick. I was so worried no one would want the valuable information I had to share because I didn't look like an Instagram influencer.

Guess what the reality was? They trusted me more. They knew it wasn't fake, I knew and lived the struggle, and we worked through it together.

A good "ideal patient" is one you not only enjoy working with – but you get to be yourself.

ACTION STEPS: Implementing The Ideal Patient Formula

Define your ideal patient using the **3-step formula.**

Adjust your website and social media messaging to match **Character Codes.**

Interview **5–10 patients** this week and use their best phrases for marketing.

Yes, this week. Pause, get out your phone – put it into your calendar.

Next Up: Understanding Marketing & Market Cycles

Now that you know **who your ideal patient is**, what makes them tick, and how to communicate with them effectively, it's time to look at **the bigger picture**—how marketing actually works in today's world.

Because let's be real: **marketing is *always* changing.**

What worked 5 years ago? Probably outdated.

What worked last year? Might be losing effectiveness.

What works *now*? That's what we're about to cover.

In Chapter 9, we'll break down:

Why marketing is constantly evolving (economics, culture, news cycles—you name it)

How to market in a "Trust Recession" when buyers are skeptical and harder to convert

The difference between a marketing cycle and a sales cycle—so you're **not** expecting instant results from the wrong strategy

Because understanding **where the market is today** is the key to making your marketing actually work.

Let's dive in!

PS – So, what do you think? Marketing *can* actually be fun, right?!? It was worth the wait (I hope!) and wading through choosing practice models, addressing mindset, offers, and pricing...

Remember the game, "Climb Higher" from Chapter 2? Step-by-step, you can do this!

Chapter 9 - Understanding Marketing & Market Cycles

Welcome to the Wild West of Marketing

If you've ever felt like marketing is an unpredictable rollercoaster, you're not wrong. One day, your strategy is working like a charm. The next, it feels like you're screaming into the void.

The good news? It's not you. Marketing is *always* changing.

The bad news? If you don't understand **why** it changes, you'll waste a lot of time and money chasing trends, guessing what works, and feeling frustrated when the thing that worked last year suddenly flops.

But don't worry—that's why we're here. This chapter is about understanding **marketing cycles**, how buyer behavior shifts, and what that means for your business **right now**.

By the end of this chapter, you'll know exactly how to adjust your marketing based on what's happening in the world, **so you don't feel like you're throwing spaghetti at the wall and hoping it sticks.**

Why Marketing is Always Changing

Marketing doesn't exist in a vacuum. It's influenced by:

- **Economics** (Are people spending or hoarding money?)

- **Culture** (What's trending? What's dying? What's making people mad?)

- **Politics** (Like it or not, elections, policies, and social movements change buying behavior.)

- **News Cycles** (A pandemic, financial crisis, or global event can change everything overnight.)

Here's an example:

Remember the early days of the pandemic? Suddenly, home workout equipment was sold out, virtual health services skyrocketed, and people were baking sourdough bread like their lives depended on it.

Fast forward a few years later, and now people are desperate for in-person experiences, travel, and **literally anything that isn't another Zoom meeting.**

Marketing shifts because **people shift.** What worked yesterday might not work today **if the market's needs, fears, and desires have changed.**

Your job isn't just to **market your business**—it's to understand **what's happening in your market.**

Marketing During a "Trust Recession"

We're living in what experts call a **"Trust Recession."**

Translation: **People trust businesses, institutions, and marketing *less* than ever.**

Thanks to shady sales tactics, over-promising, and flat-out scams, buyers are more skeptical than ever before. **And if you don't adjust your marketing to account for that, you're going to struggle.**

Here's how buyer behavior has changed:

- **People take longer to decide.** (They're researching more and comparing options.)
- **They need proof.** (Social proof, testimonials, case studies—people don't just take your word for it.)
- **They don't want to be sold to.** (Hard sells feel sketchy. Education-based marketing wins.)

How to Market in a Trust Recession:

- **Be radically transparent.** People can smell B.S. a mile away. Don't over-promise or use gimmicky sales tactics.
- **Show proof everywhere.** Use case studies, reviews, and real client results.
- **Educate first, sell second.** Teach your audience something valuable before asking for a sale.
- **Be consistent.** Showing up regularly builds trust over time.

Right now, trust is the most valuable currency in marketing. **The businesses that win are the ones who earn it.**

Marketing Cycles vs. Sales Cycles

One of the biggest mistakes business owners make is **confusing marketing cycles with sales cycles.**

Here's the difference:

Marketing Cycle = What's Happening in the Market

This is about **consumer trends, buying behavior, and the overall climate.** Are people spending freely or cautiously? Are they impulse-buying or taking months to decide?

Example:

- During economic booms, people buy fast.
- During recessions, people research more and take longer to commit.

And most importantly – how long does it take a potential patient to learn about you, move through your marketing and sign up for a no-charge consult?

Sales Cycle = How Long It Takes for Someone to Buy

This is specific to your **business model** and how long it takes for a prospect to go from "I'm interested" to "I'm buying."

Some businesses have **short sales cycles** (buying a $20 product online). Others have **long sales cycles** (investing in a $5,000 health program).

How long does it take your potential patient to sign up? It is a 1-call close? Do they need multiple calls? Do they need to purchase smaller programs or products and "test drive your services" before they buy your main patient program?

When practitioners **misread** these cycles, they make mistakes like:

- **Panicking** when sales slow down because they don't have a Plan B or C.

- **Changing their strategy too soon** before giving it time to work, because they have no metrics or KPIs they are tracking.

- **Not following up enough** with leads who just need more time to decide.

Your job? **Understand where the market is and adjust your marketing and sales cycles accordingly.**

ACTION STEPS: Identify Where Your Market is Today

1. What's happening in your industry right now?

- Are people spending freely, or are they cautious?
- Are they impulse-buying, or researching more before making a decision?
- What objections are you hearing more frequently?

2. How long is your sales cycle?

- Are people taking longer to decide?
- Do you need to follow up more?
- Are you expecting fast sales when your industry has a slow decision-making process?

3. Are you building enough trust?

- Do you have testimonials and case studies?
- Are you educating your audience instead of just selling to them?
- Are you showing up consistently, so people trust you when they're ready to buy?

Now that you understand **how public perception also impacts marketing cycles,** it's time to get tactical.

Because let's be real—knowing that people are skeptical, overwhelmed, and taking longer to make decisions is useful, but it doesn't tell you exactly **what to say** in your marketing.

That's where the **4 Marketing Angles** come in.

Next Up: The 4 Marketing Angles—How to Speak to Your Audience in a Way That Works

In **Chapter 10,** we're breaking down the **four primary ways to market anything:**

- **Pain Point Marketing** (what people are trying to escape)

- **Pleasure/Promise Marketing** (where people want to go)

- **Sale/Promo Marketing** (urgency and special offers)

- **Contrarian Marketing** (disrupting the norm)

Every successful marketing campaign falls into one (or a mix) of these four categories. **And by the end of the next chapter, you'll know exactly which one to use for your business.**

Let's dive in!

Chapter 10 - The 4 Marketing Angles Behind Everything

If you've ever felt like marketing is a never-ending mystery where some people seem to have *the magic touch* and others struggle endlessly—let me clear this up for you:

There are only four ways to market anything.

Seriously. Every single successful marketing campaign, from billion-dollar brands to the clinic down the street, boils down to one (or a mix) of these **four angles.**

The good news? **You don't have to reinvent the wheel.**

The bad news? **You do have to pick a clear message and execute well.**

Let's break down **The 4 Marketing Angles** so you can figure out which one fits your business best.

4 MARKETING ANGLES

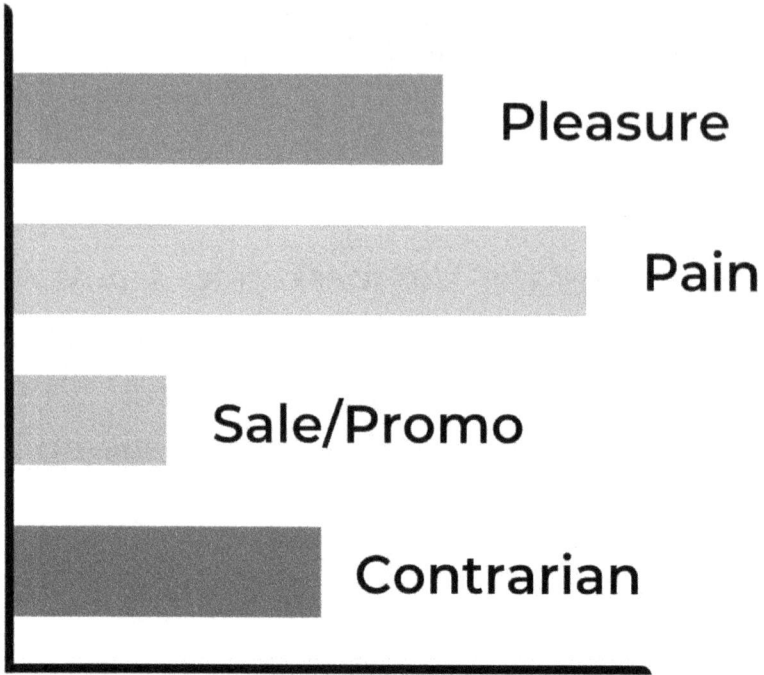

Pleasure

Pain

Sale/Promo

Contrarian

1. Pain Point Marketing – What People Are Trying to Escape

This is **the "Ouch, That Hurts"** angle.

People **buy to solve problems.** Period. Pain is the strongest motivator in human behavior. When something is uncomfortable, annoying, or downright painful enough, people **WILL pay to fix it.**

And this is where **Pain Point Marketing** shines.

How to Use It:

- Call out the pain or frustration your audience is experiencing.

- Agitate the problem a little (but don't overdo it—you're a healer, not a sadist).

- Present **your solution** as the way out of their misery.

Examples of Pain Point Marketing in Action:

"Tired of feeling bloated after every meal?"

"Sick of feeling exhausted no matter how much coffee you drink?"

"Nothing working for your stubborn weight? Here's why."

Pain Point Marketing works because **people move faster to run away from pain than they do to run toward pleasure.**

Think about it: If your hand touches a hot stove, you don't think, *"Hmm, maybe I should move my hand in a moment."* No—you yank it away immediately.

That's the power of pain.

2. Pleasure/Promise Marketing – Where People Want to Go

This is the **"Life Could Be Amazing"** angle.

While pain is a powerful motivator, **people also love to dream about a better future.** They want to believe in **transformation, results, and possibility.**

How to Use It:

- Show your audience what life could look like **if they work with you.**

- Paint a vivid picture of the benefits they'll enjoy.

- Use emotional words that make them *feel* the desire for change.

Examples of Pleasure/Promise Marketing in Action:

"Imagine waking up feeling energized, refreshed, and ready to take on the day."

"Picture yourself fitting into your favorite jeans again—without dieting or deprivation."

"What if you could finally eat without worrying about digestive issues?"

Pleasure Marketing works because people are **wired to seek out rewards.** And let's be honest—people love a **good success story.** If you can help them visualize the outcome, they'll want what you're offering.

3. Sale/Promo Marketing – Urgency & Special Offers

This is the **"Act Now or Lose Out"** angle.

There's a reason why **Black Friday, Cyber Monday, and holiday sales make people lose their minds.** Humans are irrationally driven by **urgency and scarcity.**

How to Use It:

- Offer **a time-sensitive deal** that makes people take action. (works best with hot/warm leads)
- Use scarcity (limited spots, bonuses, or discounts).
- Make it **clear why NOW is the best time** to act.

Examples of Sale/Promo Marketing in Action:

"Get 30% off your first consultation—this week only!"

"Only 3 spots left in our VIP health program. Reserve yours now!"

"This exclusive offer expires at midnight—don't miss out!"

Sales/Promo Marketing **works because humans hate missing out.** It triggers *FOMO* (Fear of Missing Out) and makes people act quickly.

But beware: **You can't use this all the time.** If every offer is a *"limited-time sale"* that never actually ends, people will stop believing you. **Use sparingly.**

4. Contrarian Marketing – Disrupting the Norm

This is the **"Wait, What?!"** angle.

Contrarian Marketing works by **challenging conventional wisdom.** People **LOVE** an underdog story, a bold opinion, or an unexpected twist that makes them rethink everything they thought they knew.

How to Use It:

- Take **a strong stance** against common industry advice.
- Challenge old ways of thinking with **a fresh, bold perspective.**
- Present your unique **solution as the "better way."**

Examples of Contrarian Marketing in Action:

"Everything you've been told about weight loss is WRONG."

"Why 'clean eating' is making your gut issues worse."

"Forget willpower—here's the real reason you can't stop sugar cravings."

Contrarian Marketing **works because people crave novelty.** If you can shake up their beliefs and show them a new perspective, they'll **pay attention.**

But a word of caution: **Make sure you have the receipts.** You can't just be contrarian for the sake of it—you need a solid argument and real proof.

Why Fitting In is Overrated (and How a Muumuu Can Make You Millions)

Contrarian marketing is basically my entire existence in business. I didn't walk into the marketing world looking like a typical "success story." No flashy watches. No sports cars. No chiseled jawline from a strict regimen of protein shakes and gym selfies. Just me, my oversized muumuu, a laptop, and a refusal to give up because I didn't fit the mold.

And guess what? **It worked.**

Why? Because standing out is the *only* way to get noticed. The internet is drowning in sameness—everyone using the same strategies, the same polished sales pages, the same "Hey, friend!" email intros. Meanwhile, I just film the videos even though I'm never ready, never polished, and half the time wearing pajama bottoms.

So, if you're worried about being "too different" in your marketing, let me remind you: **Different is good. Different is memorable. Different is what makes people stop scrolling.**

Embrace your version of the muumuu—whether that's a bold message, an unexpected take, or simply showing up as your unfiltered, real self. Because fitting in? That's the **fastest** way to get ignored.

ACTION STEPS: Choosing Your Best Marketing Angle

Now that you know the four angles, it's time to figure out **which one fits YOUR business right now** – and keep in mind you'll likely use all 4 over the course of a year – multiple times!

Ask yourself:

- What does my audience respond to best?

- What kind of messaging feels the most natural for me?

- Do I naturally lean toward **problem-solving (pain)** or **inspiring (pleasure)?**

- Does my offer benefit from **urgency (sale/promo)** or a **bold stance (contrarian)?**

- Can I mix and match angles for different campaigns?

Now, take a look at your marketing. **Which angle are you using?** And is it the one that's **actually working?**

If not, it's time to switch things up.

Next Up: Marketing Temperatures – Hot, Warm, Cold Audiences

Now that you've nailed down **your marketing angle,** the next big question is:

Who are you actually talking to?

Because not all audiences are the same. Some people are **ready to buy right now.** Others need **time, education, and trust-building.** And some? **They don't even know they need you yet.**

In **Chapter 11,** we're breaking down:

The 3% HOT buyers (ready to buy NOW – just give them the link!)

The 37% WARM buyers (interested but need more trust before pulling the trigger)

The 60% COLD buyers (not problem-aware yet – but you can turn them into future clients)

We'll also cover:

- How to structure your marketing for **each** type of audience.
- Why most people **waste** money marketing to the wrong group.
- How to move people from "never heard of you" to **"take my money!"**

If you've ever wondered why your marketing isn't landing, this is the missing piece.

Let's dive in!

PS – are you having fun yet? C'mon, isn't marketing the best!!

If you don't love it yet, just remember, learning this and mastering these skills is what leads to a full practice and the opportunity for you to serve your patients or clients.

And that connects you back to your "*why*"...remember that?

I'm having fun, I hope you are too!

PPS – if you are considering putting this book down or not reading further – hard stop. Don't run away, stop telling yourself "*I'm just not good at marketing*" or "*This is too hard.*"

Pull yourself together, sister – this is your watershed moment.

The truth is **no one** will know your ideal client better than you. They need you.

So, if you have to wade through this marketing book to be able to help those people – so be it.

Pull on those big girl panties, steel your soul, and let's go. Your mama didn't raise no sissies.

Chapter 11 - 3 Marketing Temperatures - Hot, Warm, Cold Buyers

Not All Potential Patients Are the Same (Stop Treating Them Like They Are!)

Think of marketing like online dating. You wouldn't propose marriage in your first message, right? (If you would, we need to have a different conversation.)

Yet, this is exactly how most businesses market—shouting **"Buy Now!"** at people who don't even know they have a problem.

Bad strategy.

Some people are **ready to commit right now** (HOT buyers).

Some are **interested but need time to warm up** (WARM buyers).

And some don't even know they're in the market yet (COLD buyers).

If you don't understand this, **you're leaving money on the table.**

The 3 Marketing Temperatures: Hot, Warm, and Cold

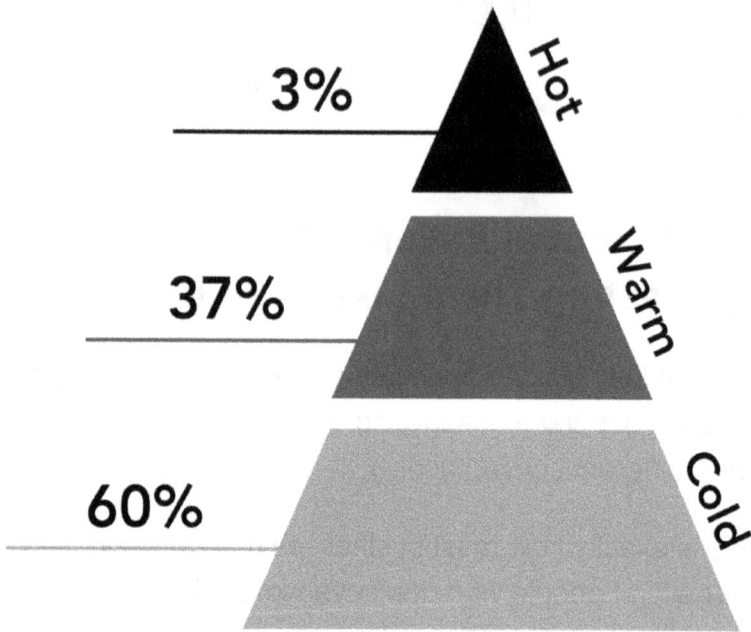

3% **Hot**

37% **Warm**

60% **Cold**

Marketing isn't about convincing people to buy—it's about meeting them where they are and moving them forward.

1. The HOT Buyers (3%) – Ready to Buy NOW

These are the "easy yes" — They already know:

- They have a problem.
- A solution exists.
- They just need to pick who to buy from.

Example of a HOT buyer:

A woman who just got lab results showing her hormones are out of whack. She's desperate to feel better and searching for a **functional medicine expert right now.**

How to market to HOT buyers:

- Make the sale easy. No jumping through hoops.
- Clear offers. "Book Your Appointment Now."
- Social proof. Testimonials, reviews, case studies.
- Urgency. "Only 3 spots left this month."

Biggest mistake?

Overcomplicating the sale.

If they're ready to buy, don't send them into a **10-email funnel.** Just give them the booking link.

2. The WARM Buyers (37%) – Interested, But Not Quite Ready

These buyers **know they have a problem** but **need more info before making a decision.**

Some are:

- Researching their options.
- Overwhelmed by choices.
- Trying to decide if it's worth the investment.

Example of a WARM buyer:

A busy entrepreneur struggling with fatigue. She's read about gut health, thyroid imbalances, and functional medicine but hasn't committed to a solution yet.

How to market to WARM buyers:

- **Educate them.** Blogs, social media, videos.
- **Build trust.** Email sequences, case studies.
- **Capture leads.** Free guides, webinars, checklists.
- **Nurture them.** Follow-up emails, retargeting ads.

Biggest mistake?

Trying to close the sale too soon.

If you pitch too aggressively, they ghost you.

3. The COLD Buyers (60%) – Not Even Aware They Have a Problem Yet

These people **aren't searching for solutions** because they **don't even know they need one.**

They just assume:

- Feeling exhausted every day is "normal."
- Bloating after meals is "just how my body works."
- Anxiety and brain fog are "part of getting older."

Example of a COLD buyer:

A high-achiever in her 40s who feels run down but **thinks it's just aging.** She has no clue her hormones, gut health, or nutrition could be causing it.

How to market to COLD buyers:

- **Problem-awareness content.** Blogs: "Why Your Fatigue Isn't Normal."

- **Engaging social media.** "5 Signs Your Gut is Wrecking Your Energy."

- **Quizzes.** "Take This 2-Minute Gut Health Assessment."

- **Low-barrier entry points.** Free resources, lead magnets.

Biggest mistake? Trying to sell to them too soon.

COLD buyers need **education first.** If you hit them with **"Buy Now"** they'll scroll right past – they are not shopping.

Don't ignore them though – this is a huge pool of potential patients, and they are your future buyers!

Why Most Practitioners Fail at This

Most practices only market to HOT buyers (3%)—and ignore the other 97%.

That's like fishing in a pond that only has three fish.

If you want **consistent** revenue, you need to:

- Attract COLD buyers and turn them WARM.

- Nurture WARM buyers until they're HOT.

- Close HOT buyers quickly and efficiently.

The Pyramid of Marketing Traffic Recap

Your audience distribution looks like this:

- 3% HOT buyers → Ready to buy now.

- 37% WARM buyers → Gathering info, weighing options, problem-aware.

- 60% COLD buyers → Don't even know they need you (yet).

If you're **only focusing on the 3%**, you're missing the **real growth opportunity**.

Smart businesses create marketing that *moves* people up this pyramid.

What Would a Middle-Aged Mama Do?

Listen, a middle-aged mama doesn't have time to build some overcomplicated, 17-step funnel that requires a team of Ivy League-educated tech bros to manage. No, we keep it simple.

The **Awareness** Funnel? That's just me showing up in my muumuu, ukulele in hand, waving like a lunatic so people *notice* me.

The **Lead** Funnel? That's inviting them onto my porch, pouring them some iced tea, and saying, "Tell me what's going on with you, hon."

The **Sales** Funnel? That's when I lean in and whisper, "I got exactly what you need, love. Let me help you fix it."

You don't need anything fancy—just a clear way to bring people in, keep them engaged, and make them an offer they *actually* want.

ACTION STEPS: Apply the Marketing Temperature Strategy

Audit your current marketing.

- Are you only targeting HOT buyers?
- Do you have content for WARM and COLD audiences? (see funnels in Chapter 14)

Map out your content plan.

- For HOT buyers: Clear offers, urgency, testimonials.
- For WARM buyers: Lead magnets, education, case studies.
- For COLD buyers: Awareness-building content, engaging social posts.

Create a marketing journey.

- COLD → WARM → HOT → BUY.

- This is how you **create sustainable growth.**

Next Up: Wave Your Flag & Build Awareness

Now that you understand **marketing temperatures** and how to speak to HOT, WARM, and COLD audiences, it's time to actually **get in front of them** and make sure they know you exist.

Because, let's be real, **no one can buy from you if they don't even know you're an option.**

In **Chapter 12,** we're diving into the **6 Ways to "Wave Your Flag" & Build Awareness**—the **most effective** methods to **reach your audience right now.**

Here's what we'll cover:

The 6 Best Marketing Channels Today (Email, Social Media, Ads, Networking, Speaking, and Affiliates)

Why Consistency Beats Complexity (doing *one* thing well is 100x better than doing *everything* poorly)

ACTION STEPS: Choosing Your Primary Marketing Method

This is **where lead generation truly starts.** If you've ever felt like you're shouting into the void and no one is paying attention—this chapter will **fix that.**

Let's go!

PS – I'm giddy with excitement – this is where you start getting your message out there. I feel like I just sucked down a helium balloon while skipping to "I Can't Fight This Feeling Anymore" by Air Supply.

Chapter 12 - 6 Ways to "Wave Your Flag" - Stop Being the Best Kept Secret

Why Visibility is Everything

Ever feel like you're amazing at what you do, but somehow, **no one knows you exist?** Like you've built this incredible practice, poured your heart into helping people, and yet… you're hearing crickets?

You're not alone.

Most practitioners struggle **not because they're bad at what they do,** but because they aren't **getting in front of enough people, enough times, in enough ways.**

You can have the best **offer, the best skills, and the best patient outcomes,** but if you don't *wave your flag* and let people **know you're here and ready to help…** your business will stay stuck.

WAVE THE FLAG
NEW PATIENTS NOW

Get the word out about the transformation you offer, who you are, how to connect with you - all leads to a CTA and most common is a NCC

eMail    Networking

Social Media    Speaking

Ads    Affiliates

That's what this chapter is all about: **getting visible.**

The 6 Ways to Wave Your Flag (And Actually Get Seen)

You don't need to **be on every platform,** run **ads 24/7,** or post **dance videos on TikTok** (unless you want to, then by all means, get it).

But you *do* need to **consistently show up** where your ideal patients or clients are already spending their time.

Below are the **6 marketing methods that are working best right now** to **create awareness and generate leads** – and the good news is you can start by just picking 1-2 and really learning to master the method.

1. Email Marketing – The Underrated Goldmine

Email is **not dead.** In fact, **it's still one of the highest-converting marketing channels.** Why?

Because unlike social media (where you're **fighting algorithms**), email is **direct.** It goes straight to your potential patient's inbox—no distractions, no random cat videos pulling them away.

How to Use It:

- **Weekly or bi-weekly emails** with valuable content, patient wins, or quick insights (ask me how/when/why you would want to email *daily*?!? Join our Facebook group **HERE** or type **https://link.thedrz.com/join-fb-group** into your url browser).

- **Automated welcome sequences** for new subscribers so they get to know you

- **Periodic promotions or special offers** to drive action

- Regular **value emails** to keep your audience engaged

If someone joins your email list, it means **they're interested in what you offer.** Don't ghost them—stay in their inbox and nurture that relationship.

PRO TIP: high value emails frequently when a new lead opts in is often a win, but **not** if every day is a sales pitch.

2. Social Media – The Visibility Engine

Like it or not, **social media is where people are hanging out.** Even if you're not personally addicted to Instagram reels or Facebook posts, **your audience probably is.**

But here's the key: **You don't have to do ALL the platforms.**

How to Use It:

- Pick **ONE** or **TWO** platforms where your audience is most active
- Post **consistently** (2–4x per week - or day depending on your goals - is plenty)
- Use a mix of **educational, engaging, and promotional content**
- Show up in **stories, reels, or live videos** to build trust faster

You don't have to be an influencer, but **you do need to be present.**

3. Ads – The Shortcut to More Leads

Want to **get in front of more people faster**? Ads are the **cheat code.**

It's easy to spend thousands, but even **a small budget ($5– $25/day)** can put your business in front of the right people **faster than organic marketing alone.**

What's most common: (see more in Chapters 15-17)

- Run **simple Facebook & Instagram ads** targeting your ideal audience

- Promote a **lead magnet (freebie, webinar, quiz) to build your email list**

- Use **retargeting ads** to bring people back to book a consultation

If done right, ads can **speed up** your lead generation *big time.*

4. Networking – The OG Marketing Strategy

Before social media, before email, before ads… **businesses grew through relationships.** And guess what? **That still works.**

People will do business with **people they know, like, and trust** if given the opportunity. That's why **strategic networking** can open doors that **no amount of social media posting ever will.**

How to Use It:

- Attend **local business events, health expos, or community meetups**

- Join **business or health professional groups** (both online & offline)

- Form **referral partnerships** with complementary practitioners (ex: a chiropractor & a functional medicine doctor; a pediatrician and a dentist) – see "Affiliates" below.

A strong network means **a steady stream of referrals and opportunities.**

5. Speaking – The Trust Accelerator

Speaking positions you as an **authority, fast.** When you're on stage (or on a podcast), people **instantly** see you as the expert.

The best part? **You don't need to be a TED Talk-level speaker to do this.**

How to Use It:

- Get interviewed on **podcasts in your niche**
- Host your own **webinars or live workshops**
- Speak at **local events, meetups, or summits**

Every speaking opportunity is a **chance to build trust and attract leads** (plus generate new content that can be repurposed!)

6. Affiliates – Let Others Market for You

What if other people **promote your business for you?** That's what **affiliates** do.

Affiliates (or JV "joint venture" partners) **recommend you to their audience**, and when someone books a consult or buys, **they get a commission or incentive.** Most physician level licenses do **not** allow for you to pay incentives, so do not reimburse for referrals of any kind, even in a non-monetary way. Seek legal advice to know the rules for *your* license.

How to Use It:

- Partner with **influencers, health bloggers, or other practitioners**
- Offer **an affiliate program for referrals** (ex: $100 per new client)
- Create **collaborative promotions or giveaways**

Affiliates can introduce you to **a whole new audience** with **zero ad spend.**

For those *unable* to pay incentives, you may be able to still set up cross-promotion relationships *without* any compensation. Check what your license legally allows.

Consistency Beats Complexity

Let's be real: The #1 reason people struggle with marketing is because they **try to do too much, get overwhelmed, and stop altogether.**

Here's the truth: **You don't need to do all 6 methods right away.**

You just need to **pick ONE or TWO, commit to them consistently,** and **do them really well.**

For example:

- If you **love writing** → Focus on **email + social media**
- If you **love talking** → Focus on **speaking + networking**
- If you **want fast results** → Focus on **ads + affiliates**

The goal is to **find what works for you,** not to burn yourself out.

ACTION STEPS: Choosing Your Primary Marketing Method

Which method feels easiest or most exciting to you? Start there.

What's your audience already engaging with? If they're on Instagram, start there. If they love podcasts, start speaking.

Commit to ONE or TWO methods for the next 90 days. Give it time to work before jumping to something new.

The key to **consistent leads** isn't doing *everything.* It's **doing the right things, over and over again.**

Next Up: How to Nurture Leads & Build Trust Over Time

So, you've waved your flag. **People know you exist.** Your social media is humming, your emails are landing in inboxes, maybe you've even had some **"Hey, tell me more about this"** conversations.

But here's the million-dollar question:

Now what?

Because here's the harsh reality—**most people don't buy immediately.**

In fact, **97% of your audience isn't ready to buy today.**

Some need more information. Some need to feel more trust. Some are interested but aren't quite sure if **you're the right fit.**

That's where **lead nurturing** comes in.

In **Chapter 13: How to Nurture Leads & Build Trust Over Time**, we'll dive into:

Lead Nurturing Strategies—How to use emails, private groups, free challenges, and **lead magnets** to stay on people's radar without feeling like a pushy salesperson.

Marketing Funnel vs. Sales Funnel—Why **just marketing** isn't enough, and how to **move people from "interested" to "I'm in."**

Setting Up Your First Nurture Sequence—Because *a lead without a follow-up plan is just a missed opportunity.*

If you've ever wondered **why people ghost after showing interest**, or how to **convert more leads into actual paying patients and clients**—this is the chapter you *do not* want to skip.

Let's build trust, create connections, and **turn more of your audience into actual customers.**

PS – this is what people mean when they say they "woke up " to an inbox full of sales or made money why they slept. Sure, that can happen – but it takes work to set it up!

Chapter 13 - How to Nurture Leads & Build Trust Over Time

The Harsh Truth About Marketing (That No One Tells You)

You put in the work.

You waved your flag.

You posted on social media, sent the emails, maybe even **got up on stage** and did a talk that had people nodding along.

And then... **crickets.**

No one bought.

No one booked.

You start questioning **everything.**

Maybe I'm just not cut out for this. Maybe my offer sucks. Maybe I should just go live off-grid and sell homemade herbal tea at a farmers' market instead.

Breathe. **You're not failing. You just need a nurturing strategy.**

Most People Need Time to Buy

Let's say you're at a party and you meet someone interesting.

You don't propose marriage five minutes in.

(I mean, you could, but it'd be weird.)

It's the same with marketing.

97% of people aren't ready to buy when they first hear about you.

- Some are curious, but not convinced.

- Some are interested, but need more information.

- Some are distracted by Netflix and will totally forget you exist tomorrow.

The **solution? Nurture them.**

Give them time to **build trust**, see the value, and **realize you're exactly what they need.**

Part 1: Lead Nurturing Strategies

How to Stay on Their Radar Without Being Annoying

You need a system that **keeps you top of mind** without feeling like a desperate ex who keeps texting, *"Hey... just checking in again!"*

Here's what works:

1. Email Marketing (Your Secret Weapon)

Your email list is **gold.**

Social media is unpredictable. Algorithms change. But **your email list is yours**—and it allows you to nurture leads **on your terms.**

The best nurture emails do 3 things:

- **Provide value.** Share quick tips, case studies, or relevant info that actually *helps* them.

- **Build connections.** Be human. Tell stories. Show them you *get* their struggles.

- **Make soft offers.** No hard sells. Just remind them you're here when they're ready.

Example: "Hey [First Name], ever feel like you're doing *everything right* and still not seeing results? I hear this all the time. In today's email, I'm breaking down why [common mistake] is keeping you stuck—and what to do instead."

People will **start looking forward to your emails** instead of deleting them.

2. Groups & Community (Your Built-In Warm Audience)

People crave **community.**

A **Facebook group, Telegram chat,** or even a **private Skool channel** can create a space where leads **engage with you** in a low-pressure way.

How to make it work:

- **Be active.** Show up consistently. Answer questions.
- **Create conversation.** Polls, Q&As, "ask me anything" sessions.
- **Give value freely.** The more you help, the more trust you build.

People love **hanging out where they feel supported.** If you create that space, when they're ready to invest in a solution, **guess who they'll go to first?**

(Yep. You.)

3. Lead Magnets & Freebies (Give Before You Ask aka Dr. Z's "Give Up Front" method)

You've seen them before:

- **"Free Guide: 10 Foods to Balance Your Hormones"**
- **"The Gut Reset Checklist"**
- **"5-Minute Stress Hack You Can Do Right Now"**

These are **lead magnets**—small, **valuable freebies** that help **capture leads** and move them into your nurture sequence.

What makes a good lead magnet?

It solves a small, specific problem. (No vague general advice.)

It's quick & easy to consume. (No 200-page eBooks, please.)

It naturally leads to your paid offer.

Example: If your paid program is about **weight loss for women over 40**, your freebie could be **"The #1 Hormonal Mistake Keeping You Stuck at the Same Weight."**

People who opt in? **They're already problem-aware**—and now you can nurture them.

Lead Magnet Magic: Using the 4 Classic Headline Templates

If your paid program is about weight loss for women over 40, your **lead magnet's headline could be**:

The Effortless Transformation Template

"How to Eliminate Stubborn Weight Without Giving Up Your Favorite Foods in Just 30 Days."

The Shortcut to Success Template

"5 Ways to Lose Weight Without Giving Up Dessert."

The Expert Elevation Template

"Lose Inches Like a Nutritionist Even Without Tracking Every Calorie."

The Resilient Roadmap Template

"Lose 10 Pounds in 30 Days—Even If You Hate Exercising."

These templates make your **lead magnets more appealing, clear, and results-driven**, increasing opt-ins and engagement.

4. Free Challenges & Mini-Workshops (Create Momentum)

If you want to **warm up leads fast**, nothing works better than **a short challenge or workshop.**

Think of it as a **low-commitment way** for people to get a **taste of your expertise** before making a bigger investment.

Example: A 3-Day Gut Reset Challenge

- Day 1: Learn what's messing up your gut
- Day 2: Try this one easy change
- Day 3: Let's talk about long-term solutions

By the end, they **see results, trust you, and want more.**

(Which is where your no-charge consult or paid offer naturally comes in.)

Part 2: Marketing Funnel vs. Sales Funnel

What's the Difference (and Why You Need Both)?

There's a **huge** mistake most practitioners make.

They think **marketing = sales.**

Wrong.

Marketing Funnel = Awareness & Trust

This is where **leads discover you, engage, and get nurtured.**

It's the emails, the social media, the groups, the free content.

Your job here? **Warm them up and build trust.**

Sales Funnel = Conversion & Action

This is where **leads move from interested to paying customers.**

- They **book a consultation.**
- They **sign up for your program.**
- They **commit to working with you.**

Your job here? **Make the offer irresistible and easy to say yes to.**

Nurture Emails: The Necessary Evil That Makes You Money

Writing nurture emails is the bane of my existence. I am a real-time, in-the-moment kind of writer. I like to *feel* the thing I'm writing about, not plan six weeks in advance like some sort of organized adult who has their life together.

But, unfortunately, winging it doesn't cut it when it comes to nurturing leads. If I relied on my moods to dictate when I emailed my list, my marketing strategy would look something like this:

- **Monday:** Feeling inspired! Writes a long, heartfelt email.
- **Thursday:** Completely forgot emails exist.
- **Saturday:** Panics, sends a random offer out of nowhere.
- **Next Week:** Wonders why sales feel inconsistent.

The reality is, people need consistent touchpoints to stay engaged. And unless I want to spend every single day manually emailing people (been there, done that), I've had to learn to *embrace* nurture sequences.

Which is why **ChatGPT is my new best friend** (see Chapter 15 for how it saves my butt daily). You think I'm sitting here cranking out nurture emails like a factory worker? Absolutely not. I let AI do the heavy lifting while I sip my hibiscus tea and pretend I'm effortlessly productive.

So, if writing nurture emails makes you want to scream into the void—just know, you're not alone. But also know that it's worth the pain. Because the more you nurture, the more people trust you. And the more they trust you, the more they buy.

Or, you know... you could just move off-grid and sell herbal teas at the farmers' market. No judgment.

ACTION STEPS: Set Up Your First Nurture Sequence

Ready to **stop losing leads** and start **turning more of them into actual clients**?

Pick ONE nurture strategy to focus on first (Email, Groups, Lead Magnets, Challenges—what fits your style?)

Map out a simple 3-email nurture sequence for new leads (Intro → Value → Soft Offer)

Check your marketing funnel. Do you have **consistent ways** for people to engage with you?

Check your sales funnel. Do you have **a clear path** for people to take the next step?

Next Up: The 3 Marketing Funnels You Need

So, now you've got your leads warmed up and nurtured like a sourdough starter that's finally ready to bake. But what happens next? How do you **actually guide people from "interested" to "invested"** in working with you?

That's where **funnels** come in. (And no, not the ones you use for pouring things into tiny bottles—though those are also useful.)

In **Chapter 14: The 3 Marketing Funnels You Need**, we'll break down:

The Awareness Funnel – How people first discover you and what makes them stick around.

The Lead Funnel – The crucial step where curiosity turns into commitment.

The Sales Funnel – The final stage that converts interest into actual paying clients.

Most people treat marketing like throwing spaghetti at a wall and hoping it sticks. **You, my friend, are going to have a system.**

Let's get strategic.

PS - before you whine about writing a 3-part email nurture sequence, I recently had to write 15 emails for two different audiences – OMG!

But it is so worth it – unless you really want to be there, every moment of the day doing manual emails in the moment. No way, Jose! We need time in life to play with goldendoodles and eat chips and guac.

Focus my friends – get those nurture emails written!

Chapter 14 - The 3 Marketing Funnels You Need

To continue the "dating" analogies – marketing funnels are like **relationship building**—you don't propose on the first date (unless you're on a reality show). Yet, **many businesses expect new leads to buy immediately** without any trust-building process.

That's why **marketing funnels exist**—to guide potential patients from "Who are you?" to "Take my money!" in a way that feels natural, builds trust, and meets them where they are.

The good news? **You only need to consider three starter funnels.** Each serves a different purpose, but together, they create a **predictable, scalable** system that **attracts, nurtures, and converts** new leads.

NOTE: While the 3 examples in the image below use a paid ad to kick off the funnel, you could use *any* of the 6 "Wave Your Flag" methods for awareness.

The Awareness Funnel: Your "Meet Cute" with New Leads

This is the **first impression**—where someone discovers your brand and **enters your ecosystem.** Maybe they found you through an ad, social media, a freebie, or a referral.

Your goal?

Capture attention

Deliver immediate value

Turn strangers into followers, email subscribers, or community members

Marketing Assets That Drive Awareness

Your audience doesn't need to know *everything* about you yet—just enough to be intrigued.

Here's how you **get on their radar:**

- **HVCO (High-Value Content Offer)**
- **What it is:** A freebie so good they'd pay for it. Think checklists, quizzes, or eBooks.
- **Why it works:** Solves a **specific** problem quickly, builds trust, and grows your email list.

Paid Marketing Funnels

Examples:

- "The Ultimate Gut Reset Cheat Sheet"

- "What's Your Health Type? Take the Quiz!"

- "5 Hidden Reasons You're Not Losing Weight"

2. Social Media Content & Organic Marketing

- **What it is:** Posts, Reels, Lives, carousels, and stories that stop the scroll and position you as the expert.

- **Why it works:** People **lurk before they buy**—a strong content game warms them up before they ever enter your funnel.

3. Low-Cost Ads & Brand Awareness Campaigns

- **What it is:** Small-budget ads that introduce your business to new audiences.

- **Why it works:** Helps reach **cold traffic** without expecting them to buy immediately.

The **Awareness Funnel** is about getting people **in the door.**

But **now what?** How do you turn awareness into action?

The Lead Funnel: Moving People from Interest to Action

Once they know you exist, you **need to nurture and build trust.**

This is where **educational marketing** shines.

People need:

Small wins before they commit

Time to see you as the **trusted expert**

Clear next steps that don't feel salesy

Marketing Assets That Move People to Action

At this stage, your audience is **curious but not convinced.** They need more education before they're ready to make a decision.

Webinars & Challenges

- **What they are:** Live or recorded deep dives on a specific topic.

- **Why they work:** Builds **authority, trust, and connection** while moving warm leads closer to buying.

Example Titles:

- "How to Fix Your Hormones Naturally (Without Guesswork)"
- "The 5 Key Pillars to Healing Chronic Fatigue"
- "10-Day Gut Reset Challenge"

2. Email Nurture Sequences (Yep, back again!)

- **What it is:** A **series** of emails that educate, inspire, and create momentum.
- **Why it works: Warms up** leads by consistently delivering **value, proof, and next steps.**
- **PRO TIP:** Make these **story-driven**—people relate more to **real experiences** than just facts.

3. Personalized Follow-Ups & Engagement Strategies

- **What they are:** Retargeting ads, DMs, or direct outreach based on behavior.
- **Why they work:** Keeps leads engaged **without being pushy.**

Example:

- "Hey [Name], saw you grabbed the Gut Reset Checklist—have you tried any of the tips yet?"

At this stage, leads are **actively considering** working with you.

But they still have questions, doubts, or hesitations. That's where the **Sales Funnel** comes in.

The Sales Funnel: Turning Warm Leads into Clients

Here's where **the biggest shift in marketing** has happened.

Old-school sales funnels relied on **pushing** people straight to a sales call.

Today?

People don't want to be "sold" on a call.

They want to feel empowered to say YES before they even book.

The Modern Sales Funnel Approach

Instead of driving traffic straight from an ad to a **high-pressure sales call**, use a **VSL Demo** that **educates, builds trust, and answers objections upfront.**

- **VSL Demo (Long-Form Video Sales Letter)**
- **What it is:** A **longer, educational** video that walks potential clients through **your process, results, and offer.**

- **Why it works better now:** With **trust at an all-time low**, leads need **more education** before buying.

- **What's Different:** Instead of "Book a Call," send them to something of value first—like a **coaching session, assessment, or roadmap.**

Example:

- "Watch this free 20-minute Gut Health Blueprint training + get your personalized roadmap."

2. Live Q&A / Consultations

- **What it is:** Instead of a high-pressure sales call, **position it as a coaching call or deep-dive session.**

- **Why it works:** Leads feel **like they're getting value, not just a sales pitch.**

3. Urgency & Risk Reversal

- **What it is:** Bonuses, limited spots, or money-back guarantees to **push people off the fence.**

- **Why it works: People procrastinate—help them decide NOW.**

$7 Million Funnel by a Middle-Aged Mama in a Muumuu

Listen, when I first heard about "digital high ticket funnels," I thought it was some complicated system designed for tech bros with whiteboards and too much caffeine. Turns out, it's just a fancy way of saying:

- Get people to notice you.
- Get them to care.
- Get them to buy.

When I built my first high ticket ad funnel in functional medicine, I didn't have a high-production video or a big ad budget. I had a Zoom call, a ukulele, and a dog who kept stealing the show. And guess what? It worked.

So no, you don't need a perfect script, an expensive software, or a photoshoot where you pretend to casually drink coffee and "work." You need to show up in a way that makes people say, *I like them. I trust them. I want to hear more.*

Because if a middle-aged mama in a muumuu can build a seven-figure funnel, **so can you.**

ACTION STEPS: Building Your Funnels: Where to Start

You don't need **all three funnels at once.**

Pick one to start:

Option 1: Create an **Awareness Funnel** with an HVCO or social content.

Option 2: Build a **Lead Funnel** using nurture emails and a webinar/challenge.

Option 3: Refine your **Sales Funnel** with a longer **VSL Demo + Coaching Call** approach.

Funnels **don't have to be complicated.** They just **need to be consistent and tested.**

Next Up: AI-Powered Marketing & How to Use Ads Effectively

Funnels are **only as good as the traffic flowing into them.** And in today's world, the smartest marketers aren't just throwing money at ads and hoping for the best—they're **leveraging AI to make every dollar work harder.**

We're diving into the future of marketing—where **AI meets advertising.**

We'll cover:

How to use AI to write high-converting marketing copy & ads (because your time is too valuable to stare at a blinking cursor).

How to use ads to amplify what's already working instead of wasting money on cold traffic that never converts.

If you're ready to work smarter (not harder) and unlock the power of AI for marketing, Chapter 15 is a must-read.

Let's dive in!

PS – I can't tell you how many times a new client would tell me – *"I've been following you for years…"*

Which is a longer time period than it took me to meet my husband, fall in love, plan a weeding, and get married.

So, I'm just saying – some people move fast and some move slow. Have a nurture process to support both of them.

Chapter 15 - AI-Powered Marketing & How to Use Ads Effectively

AI Is the Co-Pilot, Not the Pilot

Marketing used to be **gut instinct, trial and error, and a whole lot of expensive mistakes.** But today, AI can **analyze data, generate ideas, and even write marketing copy**—all while you sleep.

But let's be clear: **AI isn't replacing you.**

Think of AI as your **over-caffeinated marketing assistant**— it's fast, efficient, and occasionally spits out weird stuff that needs tweaking. **Your job?** Steer the ship, refine the message, and make sure it sounds human.

In this chapter, we'll cover:

How to use AI to write high-converting marketing copy & ads (it's finally possible!!!)

How to create an AI-powered marketing funnel that saves time!!! (goodbye, marketing chaos).

How to use ads to amplify what's already working (but not burn money on wishful thinking).

10 Tips for Using Chat GPT to Write Killer Marketing Copy

AI is only as good as **the prompts you feed it.** If you just say, "Write me an ad," don't be surprised if you get something that sounds like a bad infomercial.

Here's how to make AI work for you:

Start with a Clear Ask Be specific! Tell AI:

- **Who is your audience?**
- **What's the goal?** (Brand awareness? Lead gen? Sales?)
- **What's the tone?** (Conversational, bold, funny?)
- **What's the format?** (Ad, email, social post?)

Example: *"Write a Facebook ad for busy moms in their 40s who are struggling with low energy. Make it conversational, empathetic, and include a strong call to action to download my free guide."*

PRO TIP: Use the 3-Step Ideal Patient Formula and feed your answers into ChatGPT for even better copy!

Tell AI to Match Your Voice If you don't want it to sound robotic, paste in an example of your own writing and say, **"Match this tone."**

Give AI a Structure to Follow

- For an ad: **Hook → Pain Point → Solution → CTA**

- For an email: **Subject → Opening Story → Value → CTA**

- For a landing page: **Headline → Subhead → Benefits → CTA**

Ask AI for Variations

- "Write 5 versions of this headline."

- "Make it funnier."

- "Make it shorter."

Use AI to Brainstorm: Stuck? Have Chat GPT give you **10 post ideas, ad angles, or subject lines.**

Test Headlines & Hooks: Your first line makes or breaks engagement. **Ask AI for 5-10 hook options.**

Use AI for Storytelling: Marketing is about **stories.** Give AI the details, and it'll shape them into a compelling narrative.

Keep It Human: AI is great, but it's still **a machine.** Add **your voice, personality, and humor.**

Repurpose Content: Turn a **blog into 10 social posts.** Make an **email into an ad.** AI makes repurposing easy.

Use AI to Test & Tweak: Marketing is an **experiment.** Ask AI to generate **variations** and see what works best.

PRO TIP: Talk into AI (can add as an extension on your browser or easy enough with your phone or tablet) and have a real conversation – just talk and talk and create a long prompt. So much easier to feed in a lot of content when you are talking and not typing – then give ChatGPT (my favorite method, her name is "Sydney" and one of my favorite gal pals!) an example of how you want it to look and/or sound.

How to Create an AI-Powered Marketing Funnel That Saves Time

Funnels don't have to be **complicated.** AI makes them **faster to build, easier to optimize, and more effective over time.**

Here's how:

Step 1: Create a High-Value Content Offer (HVCO)

AI can help write **checklists, quizzes, and free guides** that attract leads.

Example: "The Ultimate Hormone Reset Checklist"

PRO TIP: In just a few hours I taught my clients how to start with a blank page and create an awesome lead magnet using ChatGPT. We used the 3-Step Ideal Patient Formula and Character Codes, so it was very customized for this doctor's audience. She ended up with a great quiz (the questions, scoring, and all the answers), marketing names for the lead magnet, the HVCO, the Facebook group, and her no charge consult, plus what kind of initial testing should likely be considered for each of the 4 archetypes. My crazy ChatGPT prompts to Sydney for the win! This can be fast!!!

Step 2: AI-Optimized Landing Page

AI can generate **headline variations, benefits, and CTAs** for higher conversions.

Example: "Struggling with exhaustion? Download the guide that's helped 5,000+ women fix their energy."

Step 3: Automated Email Nurture Sequence (Back again, like belly bloat after dinner)

AI can draft **a 5-part email series** that builds trust and warms leads.

Example Email Flow:

Welcome email – Deliver the lead magnet & share your story.

Pain point email – "Are your hormones the reason you feel exhausted?"

Case study email – Share a client success story.

Authority email – Explain why your method is different.

Offer email – Invite them to book a call or join your program.

Step 4: Long-Form VSL or Webinar

AI can help script your VSL. Also, instead of short VSLs, **longer "VSL demos"** perform better now. **Why?** More trust, more value, more conversions.

PRO TIP: Don't just push people to a sales call—give them a **quiz, assessment, or coaching session.**

Step 5: AI-Powered Retargeting Ads

AI helps **analyze which leads are warm & send them the right message.**

Example: Someone who watched your VSL but didn't book? AI serves them a testimonial ad.

AI-Generated Ad Examples That Work Right Now

Pain-Driven Ad Example *"Feeling like crap, but your doctor says you're fine?"*

- Your labs are "normal."
- Your symptoms? "Just stress."
- But you know something isn't right.

Find a practitioner who actually listens: [Insert Link]

Transformation-Focused Ad Example *"Struggling with weight, but don't know who to turn to?"*

- You've tried keto, fasting, supplements—but nothing sticks.
- Your regular doctor says, "Eat less, move more."
- You're exhausted, stuck, and over it.

Get real answers from a functional medicine expert: [Insert Link]

Story-Based Ad Example *"Your child won't eat anything but three foods. And now the rashes are starting."*

- You know this isn't "just a phase."
- You've been dismissed by doctors, judged by family, and you're out of ideas.
- It's time to find real answers.

Connect with a functional medicine practitioner today: [Insert Link]

Here are some examples I wrote and the prompt I used:

Ads I wrote for SearchFunctionalMedicine.com

Example #1:

"Feeling like crap, but your doctor says you're fine? "

Your labs are "normal." Your symptoms? "Just stress." But you know something isn't right.

You're tired of feeling awful. You're frustrated with being brushed off. And you just want someone to **listen** and **actually help**.

But where do you find them?

Your Google searches are a dead end. Local clinics only treat symptoms, not root causes. And "functional medicine" feels like a buzzword everyone's throwing around.

It's exhausting.

So, what now? Suffer in silence? Try another supplement?

Nope.

It's time to stop guessing and start searching smartly. Meet **SearchFunctionalMedicine.com**—the only platform that connects you with practitioners who actually get it.

Here's how it works:

Find **certified practitioners** in functional medicine who specialize in YOUR needs—pediatrics, hormones, gut health, autoimmune, and more.

Search for **in-person or telemedicine options** (because life is busy).

Filter by **languages spoken**—Spanish, Mandarin, French? We've got you.

Read **real patient reviews** before you book.

Know where they trained—IFM, FMA, A4M? It's all there.

It's like your secret weapon for finally finding the care you deserve.

No more guessing. No more bouncing from one "expert" to another. No more feeling stuck.

Your answer starts here.

Find your perfect practitioner now: [Insert Link]

Because you deserve to:

Feel like yourself again.

Be confident in your care.

And finally stop hearing "it's all in your head."

P.S. Don't settle for "normal" when you feel anything but. Find the practitioner who sees the whole picture—YOU.

Start your search today: [Insert Link]

Example #2:

"Struggling with weight, but don't know who to turn to? "

You've tried everything.

Keto, Paleo, Intermittent Fasting.

Gym memberships that gather dust.

Supplements that promised results but delivered nothing.

And now?

You're hearing about GLP-1 meds like Ozempic and Wegovy.

Or maybe you're thinking, *"Is there an all-natural way?"*

But who do you ask?

Your regular doctor shrugs and says, *"Eat less, move more."*

You scroll online, but the advice is either extreme or straight-up confusing.

And honestly, you're *exhausted*.

You're not lazy. You're not crazy. You're just stuck.

Because weight loss isn't one-size-fits-all.

It's about hormones. Gut health. Metabolism. Stress. Sleep.

And no diet app or "fitspo" influencer can fix that.

So, who can?

SearchFunctionalMedicine.com.

The only platform that helps you find the *right* practitioner for YOUR weight loss journey.

Here's how it works:

Need someone who can prescribe **GLP-1 medications**? We'll connect you.

Want a practitioner who specializes in **all-natural solutions**? We've got them.

Looking for someone who understands **hormonal weight gain** or the link between gut health and stubborn fat? Easy.

Prefer in-person visits or telemedicine? Your choice.

Need a provider who speaks your language? Filter for that too.

Curious about their credentials? See if they're certified by **IFM, FMA, A4M, or others.**

No more guessing. No more dead ends. Just clear answers— and the expert care you deserve.

Find your perfect practitioner here: [Insert Link]

Because let's be honest:

Weight loss isn't just about willpower.

It's not about starving yourself or sweating 7 days a week.

And it's DEFINITELY not about taking advice from TikTok.

It's about finding someone who understands YOUR body.

Your story.

Your goals.

And can finally help you see results.

So stop wasting time and energy on solutions that don't work.

Click here to find the right practitioner now: [Insert Link]

P.S. Whether you're looking for GLP-1 meds, natural solutions, or someone to finally explain what's going on with your body, SearchFunctionalMedicine.com can help. Your weight loss journey starts here.

Start your search today: [Insert Link]

Example #3:

"Can't sleep? Can't function? Desperate for help? "

You're exhausted.

You barely made it through the day on 4 cups of coffee. Your energy is gone. Your brain feels foggy. And yet—when your head hits the pillow? Wide awake.

Every. Single. Night.

You've tried:

Melatonin (like it's candy).

Warm baths (you're practically squeaky clean at this point).

Chamomile tea (one more cup and you'll scream).

And your regular doctor?

"Wear an eye mask. Avoid screens."

Thanks, but no thanks.

The idea of taking a prescription sleep med terrifies you. The zombie-like mornings? No, thank you.

But what now? You can't keep going like this.

Because the sleepless nights lead to:

Dragging yourself through the day.

Snapping at the people you love.

Constantly feeling drained, foggy, and *desperate*.

And the cycle just repeats.

Here's the truth:

Sleep isn't a one-size-fits-all problem.

It's about your hormones. Your stress. Your diet. Your habits. Your *unique* body.

You don't need generic advice. You need a solution that's tailored to YOU.

That's where **SearchFunctionalMedicine.com** comes in.

The only platform that connects you with the **right practitioner** to solve your sleep issues—for good.

Here's how it works:

Find practitioners who specialize in **insomnia and sleep disorders.**

Need someone who avoids prescription meds and focuses on **natural solutions**? Easy.

Want a practitioner who looks at your **hormones, adrenals, and stress levels**? We've got you covered.

Prefer in-person visits or telemedicine? Your choice.

Curious about their training? See if they're certified by **IFM, FMA, A4M, and more.**

Read **real patient reviews** before you book.

No more guessing. No more trial and error. No more wasting nights staring at the ceiling and days feeling like a zombie.

Find your perfect practitioner now: [Insert Link]

Because you deserve:

Peaceful, restorative sleep.

Energy and focus to tackle your day.

Solutions that work *for you*—not cookie-cutter advice.

Your answer starts here.

Click here to start your search: [Insert Link]

P.S. Sleep is the foundation of everything—your mood, your health, your LIFE. If you're tired of being tired, don't wait. Let us help you find the expert who can finally help you sleep again.

Find your practitioner today: [Insert Link]

Example #4:

"The school keeps calling. Your son's bouncing off the walls. And you're completely overwhelmed. "

You love your kiddo more than anything.

He's smart. Sensitive. Full of energy.

But lately, it feels like everything's falling apart.

The calls from the teacher. The sideways glances from other parents. The whispers about ADHD.

And now, you're lying awake at night, Googling:

"Is it really ADHD or something else?"

"What are my options beyond medication?"

"Who can actually help without blaming me as a mom?"

Because deep down, you're scared.

Scared that:

He'll get labeled as "trouble."

The school will push medication without understanding him.

The system will take away the spark that makes him so special.

And the worst part?

You feel so *alone*.

The people around you don't get it.

The teachers say, "He's disruptive." The doctor says, "Just try this prescription." The internet is full of conflicting advice that leaves your head spinning.

But what do you really want?

Someone to see your son the way you do.

Someone who'll take the time to truly understand him—his needs, his quirks, his *potential*.

Because you know there's more to this than slapping on a label or tossing pills at the problem.

You just don't know where to turn.

That's why we created **SearchFunctionalMedicine.com**.

The only platform that connects moms like you with practitioners who *get it*.

Here's how it works:

Find a functional medicine practitioner who specializes in **ADHD, behavior challenges, and pediatrics.**

Need someone who looks beyond the label? Someone who asks *why* your child is struggling? We've got you.

Looking for natural or integrative approaches? You'll find those here.

Prefer in-person care or telemedicine? Choose what works for your family. Curious about their credentials? Check if they're certified by **IFM, FMA, or others.**

Read **real reviews** from other parents before you decide.

No judgment. No shame. Just clear, compassionate help for your family.

Find the right practitioner for your child here: [Insert Link]

Because your son deserves:

A chance to thrive without losing what makes him unique.

Solutions that actually work for *him*.

Someone who listens, understands, and treats him like more than just a diagnosis.

And you, Mom?

You deserve peace of mind. You deserve to feel like you're doing the best for your child. You deserve a partner in this journey—not someone who blames you.

Start your search today: [Insert Link]

P.S. You're not alone. There's hope. And there's help. Find the practitioner who'll help your child thrive—so you both can finally breathe again.

Click here to get started: [Insert Link]

Example #5:

"Your child won't eat anything but three foods. And now the rashes are starting. "

Your little one is your whole world.

But feeding them? It's become a daily battle.

Breakfast: A tantrum. Lunch: A meltdown. Dinner: They barely touch their plate.

The foods they *will* eat? A short list of three.

And now it's not just the pickiness—it's everything else:

Constant rashes that no cream can fix.

Crying over tummy aches.

Days without a bowel movement.

Tantrums you can't explain (or control).

You're up all night Googling:

"Is it allergies? Sensitivities? Gut health?" "What's safe for them to eat?" "Why is this happening?"

You're scared. You're exhausted. And you're tired of no one taking this seriously.

The pediatrician says, *"They'll grow out of it."*

Your family rolls their eyes at another holiday meal where you bring separate food.

You're starting to doubt yourself, wondering, *"Am I just making this all up?"*

Let me stop you right there:

You're NOT imagining things.

This is real. And you're not alone.

Here's the truth:

Picky eating, food reactions, and tantrums aren't just "a phase."

They can be signs of:

Food allergies or sensitivities.

Gut imbalances.

Inflammation in the body.

Nutritional deficiencies.

And they can be *fixed*.

You just need someone who'll truly listen—someone who'll help you get to the root of the problem.

That's where **SearchFunctionalMedicine.com** comes in.

The only platform that connects parents like you with practitioners who *get it*.

Here's how it works:

Find a practitioner who specializes in **pediatric nutrition, food sensitivities, and gut health.**

Need someone who looks beyond "it's just a phase"? You'll find them here.

Prefer an integrative approach? Someone who won't dismiss your concerns? We've got you.

Choose between in-person or telemedicine care—whatever fits your schedule.

See their credentials (like certifications from **IFM, FMA, or others**) and read **real reviews** from other parents.

No judgment. No dismissiveness. Just clear, compassionate care for your child.

Find your perfect practitioner here: [Insert Link]

Because you deserve:

A child who feels good—and eats well.

Confidence in their nutrition and health.

To stop feeling dismissed and start seeing real results.

And your child?

They deserve a solution that works for *them*.

No more rashes. No more belly aches. No more guessing games about what's safe to eat.

Click here to find the practitioner who'll finally help: [Insert Link]

P.S. It's not "just picky eating." It's not "just a phase." Your instincts are right—let us help you find someone who takes them seriously and helps them thrive.

Start your search today: [Insert Link]

Example #6:

"Hormonal chaos? Labs are normal, but you feel anything but. "

You used to feel like yourself.

But now?

You're grumpy all the time. Anxious over the smallest things. The weight is piling on around your middle—and nothing seems to help.

Your libido? Gone. Your skin? Dry and dull. Your hair? Falling out in clumps.

And now, the hot flashes have started.

It feels like someone lit a fire inside you—and not in the sexy, empowered way.

You're sweating through your clothes, staring at the ceiling at 3 a.m., and wondering:

"Is this my life now?"

You tried Googling it, but the advice is all over the place:

Hormone replacement therapy?

Bioidenticals?

Supplements like wild yam?

And your regular doctor?

"Your labs are normal. Just deal with it."

But you can't *just deal with it.*

You feel like a stranger in your own body.

You're snappy with your partner, your kids, your friends. You're overwhelmed and exhausted but can't sleep. And all you want is to feel normal again.

Here's the thing:

This isn't in your head.

This is real.

And it's not just aging. It's **hormonal chaos**.

But here's the good news:

You don't have to figure this out on your own.

At **SearchFunctionalMedicine.com**, you can find the *right practitioner* to help you navigate this hormonal rollercoaster—and feel like yourself again.

Here's how it works:

Find a practitioner who specializes in **perimenopause, menopause, and hormone health.**

Need help understanding whether HRT or bioidenticals are right for you? You'll find the experts here.

Prefer natural solutions? Practitioners who combine traditional and functional medicine? We've got them.

Choose in-person care or telemedicine—whatever fits your schedule.

See their certifications (like **IFM or FMA**) and read **real reviews** from other women.

No more guessing. No more "just deal with it." No more feeling stuck.

Find your perfect practitioner now: [Insert Link]

Because you deserve:

To feel confident and vibrant in your body.

To understand what's happening—and have a clear path forward.

To finally feel like *yourself* again.

This hormonal chaos doesn't have to define you.

Start your search today: [Insert Link]

P.S. You don't have to go through this alone. There's help, there's hope, and there's a practitioner who'll take the time to understand YOU. Let's get started.

Find your practitioner here: [Insert Link]

Example of a long specific prompt:

(this is my exact prompt showing a client how to use ChatGPT – poor punctuation and all)

this is so good, I love it - the subject line for day 2 is my favorite! Can I get a 3 day email series and please make each email longer and the CTA will be to attend my "ADHD Moms vs Judgey Aunt Karen webinar" - remember really spell out the problem at the top, keep the language conversation, scannable, hit the pain points at the top and through the first section. Keep the humor in there because it makes it more relatable and easier to read. Include a section partway through that sets me up as the authority (30 years MD, dealt with my own health crisis that led to functional medicine, over half my practice is ADHD, blend the best of traditional and natural medicine) please model after this: "The school keeps calling. Your son's bouncing off the walls. And you're completely overwhelmed. " You love your kiddo more than anything. He's smart. Sensitive. Full of energy. But lately, it feels like everything's falling apart. The calls from the teacher. The sideways glances from other parents. The whispers about ADHD. And now, you're lying awake at night, Googling: "Is it really ADHD or something else?" "What are my options beyond medication?" "Who can actually help without blaming me as a mom?" Because deep down, you're scared. Scared that: He'll get labeled as "trouble." The school will push medication without understanding him. The system will take away the spark that makes him so special. And the worst part? You feel so alone. The people around you don't get it. The teachers say, "He's disruptive." The doctor says, "Just try this prescription." The internet is full of conflicting advice that leaves your head spinning. But what do you really want? Someone to see your son the way you do. Someone who'll take the time to truly understand him—his needs, his quirks, his potential. Because you know there's more to this than slapping on a label or tossing pills at the problem. You just don't know where to turn. That's why we created SearchFunctionalMedicine.com. The only platform that connects moms like you with practitioners who get it. Here's how it works: Find a functional medicine practitioner who specializes in ADHD, behavior challenges, and pediatrics. Need someone who looks beyond the label? Someone who asks why your child is struggling? We've got you. Looking for natural or integrative approaches? You'll find those here.

Prefer in-person care or telemedicine? Choose what works for your family. Curious about their credentials? Check if they're certified by IFM, FMA, or others. Read real reviews from other parents before you decide. No judgment. No shame. Just clear, compassionate help for your family. Find the right practitioner for your child here: [Insert Link] Because your son deserves: A chance to thrive without losing what makes him unique. Solutions that actually work for him. Someone who listens, understands, and treats him like more than just a diagnosis. And you, Mom? You deserve peace of mind. You deserve to feel like you're doing the best for your child. You deserve a partner in this journey—not someone who blames you. Start your search today: [Insert Link] P.S. You're not alone. There's hope. And there's help. Find the practitioner who'll help your child thrive—so you both can finally breathe again. Click here to get started:

And the results:

3-Day Email Series for ADHD Moms vs. Judgey Aunt Karen Webinar

Email 1: Subject: *"Why does it feel like everyone's judging me?!"*

Hi [Name],

Let's set the scene:

You're at a family dinner. Your child has just loudly announced they *will not* eat anything that's green, and they're currently lying under the table, refusing to come out.

Then, Aunt Karen leans in and drops the bomb: "Well, *my* kids never acted like this. Have you tried being stricter?"

Cue the boiling frustration and the urge to scream, cry, or maybe both.

It's not just Karen, is it? It's the teacher emails that keep piling up. The side-eyes from other parents at the playground. The doctor who rushed through the appointment with, "Have you considered medication?"

And then there's you: lying awake at night, thinking:

- "Am I missing something?"
- "Does my child really have ADHD—or is there more going on?"
- "Why does it feel like I'm the only one who gets him?"

You're trying *so* hard. But it's overwhelming, exhausting, and lonely.

What if I told you that you don't have to figure this out alone?

Here's What I Know (And Why You Can Trust Me)

I've been a medical doctor for over 30 years, and let me tell you—I've *seen some things*. But my perspective completely shifted when my own health crisis led me to functional medicine.

Now, over half my practice focuses on kids with ADHD. I've seen firsthand how blending the best of traditional medicine with natural approaches can transform lives.

What sets me apart?

I don't just slap a label on your child and call it a day. I dig deep to understand what's really going on.

I use a combination of evidence-based science and holistic solutions to get to the root cause.

And most importantly? I get it. I see your kid the way you do— as someone with incredible potential who just needs the right support.

Join Me For a Solution That Works

That's why I'm hosting the **"ADHD Moms vs. Judgey Aunt Karen Webinar."**

We'll cover:

- How to shut down unsolicited advice with grace (and maybe a little humor).
- The hidden triggers behind your child's behavior that no one's talking about.
- Simple, actionable steps to start improving their focus, mood, and sleep—without endless battles or side effects.

Because your child deserves to thrive without losing what makes them special. And you deserve support, not judgment.

Click here to save your seat.

P.S. Don't let Aunt Karen (or anyone else) get in your head. You're an amazing mom—and together, we'll make sure your child shines.

Email 2: Subject: *"Is it ADHD—or something else entirely?"*

Hi [Name],

The school keeps calling. Your kid's bouncing off the walls. And bedtime feels like a three-act drama with no intermission.

You've heard the whispers: "Maybe it's ADHD." "Are you going to put him on meds?" "Have you thought about a stricter routine?"

But here's the thing: ADHD isn't always the full story.

- **Could it be food sensitivities?** Certain additives, dyes, or even gluten can spark meltdowns.
- **Is it blood sugar crashes?** Many kids are more "hangry" than hyper.
- **What about nutrient deficiencies?** Low levels of magnesium or omega-3s can wreak havoc on behavior.

The truth? Every child is unique. But most doctors don't have the time—or the tools—to dig deeper.

That's where functional medicine comes in.

Why I'm Different (And Why This Matters For You)

I've been an MD for three decades, but traditional medicine alone didn't have the answers for the complex challenges kids face today.

So, I went deeper. After my own health scare, I trained in functional medicine—a field that combines the best of science with a root-cause approach to care.

Now, over half my practice is dedicated to kids with ADHD and related challenges. And here's what I've learned:

ADHD isn't "one-size-fits-all." We need to understand *your* child's unique needs.

Medication isn't the only option (and often, it's not even the best one).

Small, targeted changes in diet, environment, and habits can create huge transformations.

Ready for a Better Way?

Join me for the **"ADHD Moms vs. Judgey Aunt Karen Webinar,"** where we'll tackle:

- The sneaky triggers making your child's behavior worse.

- Why ADHD symptoms might not be ADHD at all.

- How to help your child thrive without feeling overwhelmed by all the "advice."

Save your spot here.

P.S. You've been carrying this weight on your own for too long. Let's unpack it—together.

Email 3: Subject: *"The sneaky ADHD trigger hiding in your pantry "*

Hi [Name],

Picture this: You've finally wrangled your child into the car after a chaotic morning. Breakfast was a quick bowl of cereal because *who has time?*

And then, 30 minutes later, the meltdown begins.

You're thinking:

- "What just happened?"
- "Why is this such a rollercoaster?"
- "How do other parents make this look so easy?"

Here's a little-known truth: many ADHD-like behaviors are triggered by *what your child eats*.

The Breakfast Trap

Take that quick cereal, for example. Most are loaded with sugar, which spikes your child's blood sugar fast—and crashes it even faster. That crash? It looks like hyperactivity, irritability, and impulsiveness.

What can you do instead?

Try this simple swap:

Protein-packed breakfast: Scrambled eggs with a side of fruit (berries are great for steady energy!).

Low-sugar options: Whole-grain toast with almond butter.

This one change can stabilize your child's mood and help them start the day on the right foot.

Join Me for More Game-Changing Tips

At the **"ADHD Moms vs. Judgey Aunt Karen Webinar,"** I'll share:

- What's really triggering your child's meltdowns (and how to stop them).
- My go-to strategies for improving focus, mood, and sleep—without the guesswork.
- How to navigate family dinners, school events, and life's chaos with confidence.

Because your child deserves to shine, and you deserve a plan that *actually works.*

Save your spot now.

P.S. You've got this, Mama. And I've got your back. Let's make the hard days a little easier—together.

ACTION STEPS: Start using AI Today

AI can be a game-changer for marketing, but only if you use it strategically. Here's how to start leveraging AI without losing the human touch

Set up your AI Powered Content Creation Process

Create an AI-Optimized Marketing Funnel

Use AI to Enhance Viewer Engagement

Keep it Human – Refine & Personalize

Next Up: Marketing With Feeling Words.

Now that AI is helping your marketing, It's time to integrate some feeling words into your feed that will help with eye-catching content that help move people to see what you are trying to help them with.

Chapter 16, let's go!!

PS – now that we are knee-deep in the marketing, do you see why we **had** to use so many chapters in the beginning to make sure you were clear about your 3x10 Approach, your why, your ideal client, your offer…

Building a business isn't for wussies – but guess what, **you are stronger than you think!** And when you know why you are doing this, then this all just becomes some of the hoops you jump through on the way to success.

And here's a good reality check – everyone **has** to work. You work a job, you work running a house – **life is work.**

So, why not make it where you *choose* the work and get to build the life you want? Clearly, I'm a fan. If you need someone to believe in you, I've got you.

Chapter 16 - How to Supercharge Your Marketing with Feeling Words

Words matter.

They have the power to **grab attention, evoke emotion, and drive action.** The right words can make the difference between an ad that gets scrolled past and one that stops someone in their tracks. Between an email that gets deleted and one that gets opened, read, and clicked.

This is where **Feeling Words** come in.

These are the high-impact, emotionally charged, action-oriented words that make your marketing more persuasive, engaging, and effective. They create a sense of urgency, credibility, and excitement—without resorting to gimmicks or over-the-top sales tactics.

Think of them as **marketing fuel**—they ignite curiosity, trust, and momentum in your audience.

But here's the secret: **Feeling Words work best when they're used strategically.** Too many and your message sounds forced. Too few and it falls flat. The goal is to weave them into your copy naturally, making it more compelling without losing authenticity.

To make it easy, I've categorized **300 of the most effective Feeling Words** below. Use them to level up your emails, ads, social media, and website copy. Whether you need to create **urgency, establish credibility, or trigger an emotional response**, you'll find the right words here.

First, they are listed alphabetically for when you need to name something and need it to start with an "R" or a "P".

Then you can scroll through the Feeling Words by the emotion/action/feeling they drive such as: curiosity, urgency, action, trust, sensory, etc.

Alphabetical Feeling Words:

Accelerate	Alert	Authentic
Accessible	Amazing	Awe-inspiring
Accomplish	Amplify	Bargain
Achieve	Anniversary	Bargain
Act now	Announcing	Beautiful
Advantage	Approved	Before it's gone
Advice	Astonishing	Beginner-friendly
Affordable	Astounding	
Alarming	Attractive	Best

Best-selling	Compare	Discount
Better	Competitive	Discover
Big	Complete	Don't miss out
Blissful	Compromise	Drive
Bonanza	Confidential	Easily
Bonus	Conquer	Easy
Boost	Controversial	Edge
Bottom Line	Crammed	Effortless
Breaking	Create	Elite
Breakthrough	Crisp	Emerging
Breathtaking	Daring	Empower
Bright	Dazzling	Endorsed
Captivating	Delicious	Energize
Catapult	Delighted	Energy
Certified	Delightful	Enhance
Challenge	Delivered	Enormous
Champion	Dependable	Enthralling
Colorful	Destiny	Enviable
Colossal	Direct	Excel

Excellent	Gigantic	How-To
Exciting	Gleaming	Huge Gift
Exclusive	Glowing	Hurry
Exhilarating	Greatest	Hurry
Exploit	Growth	Ignite
Extra	Guarantee	Imagination
Extraordinary	Guaranteed	Immediately
Fascinating	Hassle-free	Important
Feel secure	Health	Improve
Final chance	Heartwarming	Improve
First	Help	Improved
Focus	Helpful	Improvement
Forbidden	Hidden	Increase
Fortune	High Tech	Incredible
Fragrant	High-end	Informative
Free	Highest	Innovative
Full	Honest	Insider
Fundamentals	Hot	Inspires
Genuine	Hot Special	Instructive

Interesting

Introducing

Intuitive

Ironclad

It's Here

Jaw-dropping

Jumpstart

Just Arrived

Know

Largest

Last Chance

Last Minute

Last opportunity

Latest

Launching

Lavish

Lavishly

Learn

Legitimate

Liberal

Lifetime

Limited

Limited availability

Limited edition

Little-known

Lose weight

Love

Lowest

Luminous

Luxurious

Luxury

Magic

Mainstream

Mammoth

Manageable

Master

Mind-blowing

Miracle

Money

Monumental

More

Motivating

Must-have

New

No-fuss

Noted

Now

Now or never

Obsession

Odd

Off-limits

Offer

Once in a lifetime

Opportunities

Opulent

Outstanding	Proven	Revisited
Overcome	Provincial	Revolution
Pain-free	Punctual	Revolutionary
Painless	Quality	Reward
Perspective	Quick	Risk-free
Pioneering	Radiant	Running out
Popular	Rare	Safe
Portfolio	Rarity	Safety
Powerful	Realize	Sale
Practical	Reduced	Sampler
Premier	Refreshing	Scarce
Prestigious	Refundable	Scarcity
Prevail	Reliable	Seamless
Professional	Reliable	Secret
Profit	Remark	Secure
Profitable	Remarkable	Security
Promising	Results	Select
Promote	Results-driven	Selected
Protect	Revealing	Selling fast

Sensation	Thrive	Upgrade
Sensational	Time-sensitive	Uplift
Shocking	Top-secret	Upscale
Simple	Top-tier	Urgent
Simplified	Transform	User-friendly
Smooth	Triumph	Value-packed
Sneak peek	Trusted	Verified
Sophisticated	Unbelievable	Vibrant
Sparkling	Uncomplicated	Walkthrough
Spellbinding	Uncover	Warranted
Straightforward	Unleash	Warranty
Streamlined	Unlock	World-class
Stress-free	Unmatched	Worry-free
Supercharge	Unparalleled	Worthwhile
Surpassing	Unsurpassed	Zero-risk
Tested	Untold	Zinger

Feeling Words categorized into different themes such as **action-oriented**, **persuasive**, **emotional trigger**, **sensory**, **urgency**…

Action-Oriented Words

- Accelerate
- Accomplish
- Achieve
- Act now
- Amplify
- Boost
- Catapult
- Create
- Drive
- Energize
- Empower
- Enhance
- Ignite
- Improve
- Jumpstart
- Master
- Optimize
- Propel
- Supercharge

- Transform
- Unleash
- Upgrade
- Uplift
- Thrive

Persuasive Words

- Advantage
- Affordable
- Best-selling
- Exclusive
- Guaranteed
- Proven
- Risk-free
- Reliable
- Safe
- Secure
- Special Offer
- Verified
- Trustworthy
- Winning
- Results-driven
- Results
- Professional

- Highest
- Premium
- Top-tier
- Legitimate
- Reputable
- Dependable
- Endorsed

Emotional Trigger Words

- Amazing
- Astonishing
- Awe-inspiring
- Blissful
- Captivating
- Delightful
- Delighted
- Enthralling
- Exhilarating
- Fascinating
- Heartwarming
- Inspirational
- Jaw-dropping
- Motivating
- Mind-blowing

- Remarkable
- Sensational
- Shocking
- Spellbinding
- Thrilling
- Unbelievable
- Wonderful

Sensory Words

- Aromatic
- Bright
- Crisp
- Delicious
- Dazzling
- Fragrant
- Gleaming
- Glowing
- Luminous
- Radiant
- Refreshing
- Smooth
- Sparkling
- Velvety
- Vibrant

- Silky

Urgency and Scarcity Words

- Before it's gone
- Don't miss out
- Final chance
- Hurry
- Last Chance
- Last Minute
- Limited availability
- Limited edition
- Now or never
- Once in a lifetime
- Running out
- Selling fast
- Time-sensitive
- Urgent
- While supplies last
- Zero-risk

Trust and Security Words

- Certified
- Confidential
- Dependable

- Endorsed
- Genuine
- Honest
- Ironclad
- Legitimate
- Proven
- Reputable
- Secure
- Tested
- Trusted
- Verified
- Warranty
- Safe
- Secure

Curiosity-Inducing Words

- Hidden
- Insider
- Little-known
- Off-limits
- Secret
- Sneak peek
- Top-secret
- Unmatched

- Unparalleled
- Untold
- Unrevealed
- Unlock
- Unveil

Success and Achievement Words

- Accomplish
- Champion
- Conquer
- Excel
- First
- Focus
- Fortunate
- Master
- Overcome
- Prevail
- Prosper
- Realize
- Succeed
- Surpass
- Triumph
- Win

Simplicity and Ease Words

- Beginner-friendly
- Effortless
- Easy
- Hassle-free
- Intuitive
- Manageable
- No-fuss
- Painless
- Simple
- Smooth
- Straightforward
- Stress-free
- User-friendly
- Walkthrough

Exclusivity and Prestige Words

- Elite
- Exclusive
- High-end
- Lavish
- Luxury
- Opulent
- Premier

- Prestigious
- Rare
- Select
- Sophisticated
- Top-tier
- World-class

Other Powerful Words

- Affordable
- Announcing
- Anniversary
- Bonus
- Bottom Line
- Breaking
- Complete
- Competitive
- Discount
- Discover
- Edge
- Emerging
- Enormous
- Exciting
- Extraordinary
- Fascinating

- Fortune
- Free
- Full
- Fundamentals
- Gigantic
- Greatest
- Health
- Help
- Helpful
- Hot
- Hot Special
- Huge Gift
- Immediate
- Important
- Improve
- Innovative
- Instructive
- Introduce
- Just Arrived
- Know
- Largest
- Latest
- Lavishly

- Lifetime
- Limited
- Love
- Lowest
- Magic
- Miracle
- Monumental
- More
- New
- Noted
- Opportunities
- Outstanding
- Powerful
- Practical
- Profitable
- Promising
- Promote
- Proven
- Quality
- Quick
- Reduced
- Results
- Revolutionary

- Sale
- Sampler
- Scarce
- Selections
- Seamless
- Selected
- Selling Fast
- Simple
- Simplified
- Supercharge
- Tested
- Time-sensitive
- Top-secret
- Trusted
- Unbelievable
- Uncomplicated
- Unveil
- Upgrade
- Upscale
- Verified
- Worry-free
- Worthwhile

Why "Feeling Words" Matter (And Why Chad Would Probably Call Them 'Synergy Triggers')

Look, I get it. This whole thing sounds like something cooked up in a corporate boardroom by a guy named Chad who drinks protein shakes and yells *"Let's circle back!"* in meetings.

But here's the thing—words **do** matter. A lot.

The right words make people *feel* something. And when people feel something, they take action. That's why I call it **"Feeling Words."** Because that's exactly what they do—they trigger emotions, spark connection, and make your message land in a way that actually resonates.

But let's be real: Some marketing words are **so overused they make people cringe.** If I see another ad promising something *"revolutionary"* or *"game-changing,"* I might throw my laptop into the sea. (Full disclosure: I've used both of these lol!)

So, here's my rule: **Use Feeling Words like seasoning.** A little? Chef's kiss. Too much? You've turned your message into an overcooked, inedible mess.

And if you ever feel awkward using them, just remember: Some dude out there is selling a $97 scented candle with *"soul-nourishing, aura-altering tranquility."*

If he can do that, you can confidently use words that actually help people connect with what you do.

ACTION STEPS: The Power of Words in Marketing

Audit Your Existing Marketing Copy: Review your content on your social media and other platforms to see if any of the wording can be improved.

Optimize Your Key Marketing Materials with Feeling Words: Check to see if you have urgency and trust words in your copy.

Create a Feeling Word Swipe File: Select your favorite feeling words from above and add them to the list. Keep the file fresh and updated when you find other words that appeal to you.

Run A/B Tests for Different Word Choices: take the same post and put it in different groups with slightly different copy to see which one performs better.

Next Up: The Reality Check About Running Ads

If you've ever thought, **"I should probably run ads, but I have no idea where to start"**—you're not alone.

Here's the truth: **Most practitioners never run paid ads, and that's okay!**

But for those who do, the difference between **wasted money** and **a thriving practice** comes down to **strategy, timing, and knowing what you're getting into.**

In **Chapter 16**, we're breaking down:

Why most practitioners never touch paid ads (and why that might be a good thing).

When to go organic vs. when to pay for traffic—so you don't burn money before you're ready.

What you absolutely MUST know before hiring an ad agency (because getting this wrong can cost you big).

How to decide if ads are the right move for your practice— right now or later.

If you've been **curious about ads but unsure if they're worth it**, this chapter will give you the **clarity you need to make a smart decision.**

Let's dive in!

Chapter 17 - The Reality Check About Running Ads

Why Most Practitioners Never Run Paid Ads (And That's Okay!)

Ah, ads. The thing every marketing "guru" tells you is the missing piece between you and the flood of patients who will have you booked out for months.

But if you've been in business for any amount of time, you already know the truth: **ads can be expensive, tricky, and—if done wrong—a money pit.**

The reality? **Most practitioners don't actually need to run paid ads right away** (if ever). Many practices get to multiple 6- or even 7-figures without ever touching Facebook Business Manager. Instead, they focus on **organic growth strategies**— things like referrals, content marketing, and networking.

And here's the real kicker: **if you don't have a strong foundation in place, ads won't save you.** They'll just amplify what's already happening (for better or worse).

So, before we even **talk** about running ads, let's take a step back and make sure you're really ready.

Organic vs. Paid: When Should You Spend on Ads?

Let's play a little game. Answer these questions honestly:

1. Do you have a clear **offer** that people actually want? (This means you are already selling it too!)

2. Are you **booking clients consistently** through organic methods?

3. Is your messaging **clear, compelling, and conversion-friendly**?

4. Do you have a **proven process** for turning leads into paying clients?

If you answered "yes" to *all* four, congrats! You're **ready to amplify what's working with ads** (not fix what's broken).

If you answered "no" to one or more…hold off on ads for now. **Fix the leaks in your marketing and sales systems first.** Otherwise, ads will just pour more water into a broken bucket.

How 6-, 7-, and 8-Figure Practices Approach Marketing & Sales

Every practice has a different approach to marketing and sales depending on where they are in their growth journey.

6-Figure Practices: The Operator Stage

Your role:

You're doing everything—practitioner, marketer, salesperson, admin.

Marketing focus: Scrappy, organic growth. You're posting on social media, writing emails, relying on word-of-mouth, and manually following up with leads.

Sales strategy: You're personally handling every sales call and making it up as you go. There's no set script, just pure hustle.

Biggest challenge?

You're trading time for money, and growth is limited because you can't scale yourself.

Marketing Strategies That Work Best for You:

High-Value Content Offers (HVCOs)— eBooks, checklists, quizzes to attract leads

Personal networking & community-building—referrals, collaborations, social proof

One-to-one sales efforts—no fancy automation, just direct conversations

7-Figure Practices: The Manager Stage

Your role: You're managing a team, delegating, and creating systems.

Marketing focus: You start investing in **paid ads, automated funnels, and strategic partnerships.** You're not just getting clients—you're **nurturing and scaling.**

Sales strategy: You have a **repeatable process** for converting leads, maybe even a sales team handling consult calls.

Biggest challenge? Letting go of control and trusting your team to execute.

Marketing Strategies That Work Best for You:

Webinars & evergreen content—automated nurturing & education

Paid ads (strategically!)—targeted traffic to tested funnels

Automated email sequences—nurturing leads on autopilot

8-Figure Practices: The Founder Stage

Your role: You're the visionary, focused on growth, innovation, and brand-building.

Marketing focus: You're **dominating your niche** with high-level partnerships, major ad campaigns, and **omnipresent** brand positioning.

Sales strategy: You've built a **well-oiled machine** where your team runs everything, and you step in for **big opportunities.**

Biggest challenge? Scaling without losing quality and staying innovative in a competitive market.

Marketing Strategies That Work Best for You:

Brand-level marketing—large-scale campaigns, strategic partnerships

Multi-channel advertising—Google, YouTube, social, TV, and PR

High-ticket sales process—automated funnels for premium clients

So, where are you right now?

Operator?

Manager?

Founder?

And more importantly—where do you *want* to be?

What You Need to Know BEFORE Hiring an Ad Agency

If you're at the **7-figure Manager stage and beyond,** you might be thinking about hiring an ad agency. **But proceed with caution.**

Red Flags to Watch For

They promise "overnight" results.

They have zero experience with healthcare or your niche.

They don't ask about your business goals before pitching a strategy.

They suggest running cold traffic ads when you don't even have a proven offer yet.

Better Approach: Find an agency or expert who:

Understands **functional medicine, wellness, or healthcare** marketing.

Focuses on **data-driven testing** instead of "quick wins."

Helps you refine your **messaging, landing pages, and follow-up process** (not just run traffic).

Has a **proven track record** of working with businesses like yours.

PRO TIP: If you're not quite ready to invest in an agency, **start small with self-managed ad campaigns.** Learn the basics, test a few audiences, and optimize before going all-in.

My $7 Million Zoom Secret – Lipstick

People don't need perfection. They need *connection.* You don't have to be a 27-year-old with a six-pack and a ring light to sell something. (And thank God for that, because at this point, my six-pack is just the herbal shots in my fridge.)

So, if you've been waiting to "look the part" or "get it just right" before launching your marketing, stop. Show up as you are. If this middle-aged mama can do it, so can you.

ACTION STEPS: Deciding If Ads Are Right for Your Practice

Still unsure whether to run ads? Let's make it simple:

Run ads if:

You have a **proven** offer that converts organically.

You have **systems in place** to handle lead follow-up and sales.

You're ready to **invest consistently** (not just "try it out" for a month).

Don't run ads if:

You don't have a **clear** marketing strategy.

Your current **organic** marketing isn't working.

You think ads will magically "fix" a broken business model.

Your best move right now?

If you're a **6-figure Operator,** focus on organic growth and referrals.

If you're a **7-figure Manager,** start small with targeted ads to amplify what's already working.

If you're an **8-figure Founder,** build a high-level paid ad strategy to dominate your niche.

Next Up: Quickstart 6 Weeks to $30k

Ever curious how to generate some cash quickly in practice to fund a project, hire a staff member, or maybe have the money to run ads…WITHOUT needing to get a business loan?

Chapter 18 will show a simple formula for how. Our clients have used it again and again. Want to know more fast-start plans for funding? Pop into our Facebook group and tag me Join **HERE** or type **https://link.thedrz.com/join-fb-group** into your url browser.

Let's do this!

PS – I can teach you how to market and make money -but one of the fastest ways I can help you is teaching where not to WASTE money. Reread this chapter before going half-cocked on ads…thank me later.

Chapter 18 - Quickstart Guide 6 Weeks to $30k Retention

How to Generate Revenue Fast Without Needing a Loan

Step One: Get into Action—But Not Just "Busy" Work

There's a huge difference between **being busy and being productive** when it comes to hitting a revenue goal fast. If you've ever spent a whole day tweaking your website font, scrolling Instagram for "inspiration," or endlessly brainstorming your perfect offer (without actually talking to a single lead), **this section is for you.**

To hit **$30K in 6 weeks,** you need to master **three things FIRST:**

Marketing – Bringing in potential patients aka "Find a Patient"

Sales – Converting them into paying clients aka "Sign a Patient"

Fulfillment – Delivering excellent care that leads to renewals, referrals, and retention aka "Serve a Patient"

"Find, Sign, and Serve a Patient" – this is the *minimum* to master to have <u>Proof of Concept</u> and know that you *can* do this!

This is **not** the time for perfectionism. It's the time to get into **focused action.**

The $30K in 6 Weeks Plan

This formula is simple, repeatable, and **it works.** Sometimes you need a big goal in a short amount of time to see what *you* can accomplish.

FOCUS: One Offer, One Message, One Launch

If you want to scale quickly, **you need to get known for one thing.**

No throwing ten different offers out there.

No launching three different services at once.

No reinventing your business every other week.

Example: A **6-week gut reset program** at **$5,000 per patient**.

Goal: Sign **6 new patients** at $5K each = **$30K.**

Stick with **one** marketing message, **one** launch strategy, and **one** offer.

FAMOUS: Tell Everyone & Leverage Groups

This is not the time to be shy. **You need to get loud.**

Email your list (even if it's small).

Post on social media daily.

Leverage groups, podcasts, and local networks.

Reach out personally to past patients or warm leads.

Remember: People don't buy what they don't know exists. You **have** to put your offer in front of them—**multiple times.**

PRO TIP: use a simple funnel, drive leads to a webinar, from there invite them to a No Charge Consult (NCC) and then sign them up.

FOLLOW-UP: Do More Sales Calls Than You Think You Need

If you're not booking **at least** 24 sales calls in the next 6 weeks, you're **not** having enough conversations.

The biggest mistake people make? **They assume if someone is "interested," they'll reach out. Nope.**

You **must** follow up.

In a week: 12 calls → Convert **3** patients.

Following week: 12 more calls → Convert **3** more patients.

That's **6 new patients = $30K.**

PRO TIP: If you're struggling to book calls, **personally invite people** instead of waiting for them to come to you.

FORMAT: The Simple Weekly Breakdown

Here's **exactly what your next 6 weeks could look like:**

Week 1-2: Plan & prep—create your marketing content, email sequences, and outreach list.

Week 2-3: Launch—run a webinar, challenge, or direct outreach.

Week 3: Sales Calls (12 calls, 3 new patients).

Week 4: More Sales Calls (12 calls, 3 new patients).

Week 5: Deliver your program while continuing marketing & sales (back up time to hit your goals)

Week 6: Continue nurturing leads & sales for your next cycle.

This **works** because you're combining **high-intent marketing with high-touch sales.** You have to do the work though and hit your goals – if you *say* you are going to book 12 sales calls in a week, then you must do the work to make that happen.

Patient Renewals, Retention & Monthly Recurring Revenue (MRR)

Once you've hit **$30K in 6 weeks**, and you have patients working through a program, what's next? You don't want to start over from scratch every time. This is where patient **renewals, memberships, and subscriptions** come in.

Patient Renewals – Keeping Clients Engaged

Most people don't hit their health goals in just one cycle. The key to **sustainable revenue** is **offering renewals and continued care.**

- **Set the stage early:** Let them know in their first visit that health is a long-term process.

- **Use progress milestones:** Show them where they started vs. where they are now.

- **Offer renewal incentives:** Give discounts or added bonuses for committing to another phase.

Example: After a 5-month intensive for $4995, but more work still needed, they could do another 5 months for $2450 with less visits. Or maybe they are ready for a maintenance plan at $297/month.

Membership Models – Predictable Monthly Revenue

If you want to **remove the feast-or-famine cycle**, consider a membership program.

Example: A **$97/month wellness membership** that includes:

- Monthly Q&A group calls
- Discounts on supplements & lab testing

- Ongoing educational content

100 members x $97 = $9,700/month in passive revenue.

Subscription-Based Income – Easy, Scalable Revenue

Want **recurring income with minimal effort?** Set up a subscription.

Examples:

- **Supplement Auto-Ship** – A monthly gut repair kit delivered to their door.

- **Lab Testing Packages** – Annual lab reviews for long-term care.

- **Meal Plans & Guides** – New recipes, workouts, or health tips each month.

The more **predictable revenue you create,** the **more stability your practice will have.**

Key Differences Between These Concepts

Key Differences Between These Concepts

Aspect	Renewals	Retention	Memberships	Subscriptions	MRR
Focus	Continuation of care after a program	Keeping patients engaged over time	Ongoing access to services/perks	Delivery of specific recurring products/services	Revenue generated from all recurring models
Primary Benefit	Ensures long-term care and results	Builds loyalty and trust	Steady revenue + high perceived value	Convenience + automated income	Financial stability and predictability
Common Models	Program extensions, maintenance visits	Follow-ups, exclusive perks	Monthly wellness plans, VIP clubs	Supplements, labs, digital content	Combined revenue from memberships, subscriptions, and renewals

How to Integrate These Strategies into Your Practice

These are things to consider – you don't need to do them all!

Step 1: Start with Renewals and Retention

Build the foundation for long-term patient relationships by setting expectations early and maintaining consistent communication.

Step 2: Layer in Memberships

Create tiers to cater to different needs, such as a **basic plan for ongoing education** and a **premium plan with direct access to services.**

Step 3: Add Subscriptions for Easy Wins

Offer **auto-renew options for supplements, labs, or meal plans.** Patients love the convenience, and you'll love the recurring income.

Step 4: Focus on Building MRR

Combine **memberships and subscriptions** into a **unified offering** that maximizes value for patients while generating reliable income for your practice.

PRO TIP: When practitioners sell their practice (this might be your exit strategy) they often sell "good will" which is the patient base they had, but aside from real estate or equipment, there isn't a tangible value which makes it very difficult for banks to provide a loan to the new practice buyer. Build MRR into your practice and that provides a real valuation that makes your practice more lucrative and appealing to lenders.

You Mean I Have to Actually Talk to People?

Listen, I'd love to tell you that you can hit $30K in 6 weeks by rearranging your desk, color-coding your calendar, and manifesting clients with a vision board. But nope. Turns out, you actually have to talk to people. Like real, live humans.

I know—it's tragic.

I spent a solid six weeks once, deeply engrossed in the "preparing" phase, convincing myself that my email sequence needed *just one more* tweak before I could *possibly* start selling. (Spoiler alert: That was just procrastination wearing a productivity hat.)

The truth? The fastest way to make money in your business is to **have more conversations.** That's it. No fancy hacks, no complex funnels—just real, actual conversations where you invite people to work with you.

You don't have to sound perfect. You don't have to have a Hollywood-level sales script. You just have to *get out there and do the thing.*

And if that makes you nervous? Well, welcome to the club. I'll be right there with you, sweating through my muumuu, psyching myself up before a sales call like I'm about to go into battle.

But guess what? Every awkward, slightly-too-long pause is worth it. Because those conversations? That's where the magic happens.

Now, stop stalling and go book some calls. You've got this.

ACTION STEPS: Implementing the 6-Week Plan

- **Pick one medium or high-ticket offer** (ex. 3-5 months, $3K to $7500 price point).
- **Set a revenue goal** (ex. $30K = 6 clients at $5K each).
- **Choose your marketing strategy** (webinar, challenge, direct outreach).
- **Book 24+ sales calls** (aim for 6 new patients).
- **Plan renewals, memberships, or subscriptions** to turn quick cash into long-term income.

Next Up: Avoiding Common Marketing Mistakes

You're rolling. You've got the roadmap to hit $30K fast. Now let's make sure you don't waste time and money on the biggest marketing mistakes that kill results.

In Chapter 19, we'll cover:

- **The top 5 ways practitioners waste money on marketing.**

- **How to fix marketing leaks and boost conversions.**

- **Action steps to plug any holes in your marketing strategy.**

Before you launch anything else, let's make sure your marketing is airtight.

PS – wondering if the Quickstart 6 Weeks to $30k is real? It is. I've done it (many times) and so have many clients. It's not casual though, you have to be **focused** and **drive** it. (Go back and read Chapter 1)

I dare you to try it. Double dog dare you.

Because once you learn this skill, you are **unstoppable**. Like scary capable, like you're Neo and chose the red pill.

You'll essentially become your own bank, capable of generating income as needed. Just remember at a minimum you must "find, sign, and serve" that client.

Chapter 19 - Avoiding Common Marketing Mistakes

Why This Chapter Matters

Marketing is **critical** for business success, but it can also be a massive **money pit** if you're not strategic. Most practitioners waste **thousands** of dollars (and hours) on marketing that doesn't generate revenue.

You don't need to **spend more** on marketing. You need to **spend smarter.**

Let's talk about the **top five mistakes** that are draining your budget—and how to fix them.

The Top 5 Marketing Money Wasters (And What to Do Instead)

1. Running Ads Too Soon (Before You Have a Proven Offer)

The Mistake: Jumping into Facebook or Google Ads **before** you have a dialed-in offer, sales process, or proven messaging.

The Reality: Ads amplify **what's already working.** If your marketing isn't converting organically, paid ads won't magically fix it.

The Fix:

- Start with **organic marketing** (social media, email, networking) first.
- Make sure your offer **actually sells** before throwing money at ads.
- Use **retargeting ads** on warm leads, not cold traffic.

PRO TIP: Test your messaging by running a **free challenge or webinar** before launching a paid ad campaign.

2. Trying to Be Everywhere (Without a Strategy)

The Mistake:

Posting on **every** platform (Instagram, Facebook, LinkedIn, TikTok, YouTube, Pinterest…) and burning yourself out **without a clear strategy.**

The Reality:

More platforms = More work.

Spreading yourself too thin **dilutes** your marketing impact.

The Fix:

- **Pick 1-2 core platforms** where your audience actually hangs out.

- Go **deep** instead of wide—post **valuable** content consistently.

- **Repurpose content** instead of reinventing the wheel every day.

PRO TIP: Record **one** long-form video and repurpose it into **reels, blog posts, and emails** instead of creating new content from scratch.

3. Ignoring Lead Nurture (Not Following Up Enough)

The Mistake:

Only focusing on **getting leads** but **not following up** enough to convert them into paying clients.

The Reality: Most leads need **multiple touchpoints** before they buy. If you don't nurture them, they'll forget about you.

The Fix:

- Set up a **3-5 email nurture sequence** for every new lead.

- Use **retargeting ads** to stay in front of warm leads.

- Send a **weekly email newsletter** with value + a soft pitch.

PRO TIP: Leads don't **remember** you unless you stay in touch. Don't be afraid to **connect multiple times**—people need reminders!

4. Focusing on Features Instead of Outcomes

The Mistake:

Marketing your **services and credentials** instead of selling **outcomes and transformations.**

The Reality:

People don't care about your fancy degrees or lab tests. They care about **how their life will change.**

The Fix:

- Speak **to their pain points and desires**—not just your services.

- Use **social proof** (testimonials, case studies) to show results.

- Sell the **end result** (better sleep, more energy, weight loss)—not the process.

PRO TIP: Your **headline matters**—make it outcome-driven, like:

"How to Lose 10 Pounds in 30 Days—Without Counting Calories."

5. Not Automating (Wasting Time on Repetitive Tasks)

The Mistake:

Manually doing **everything**—posting content, following up with leads, scheduling calls—when automation could save hours every week.

The Reality: You can **automate 80% of your marketing** without losing the personal touch.

The Fix: Automate:

Email sequences for new leads

Social media scheduling

Lead capture & follow-up

Appointment booking & reminders

Ad retargeting

PRO TIP: The more you automate, the **more time** you have to focus on **sales and patient care.** Use FMA Marketing and all of our built-in funnels and automation. You can see it **HERE** or type **https://thedrz.com/functional-medicine-automation/** into your browser url.

Automating Your Marketing: What Can You Get Off Your Plate?

Marketing **doesn't** have to be a full-time job.

You can automate and **delegate** key tasks so your marketing works 24/7—without you lifting a finger.

Fully Automate These Marketing Tasks

1. Email Marketing (Your #1 Automation Priority)

Welcome sequences → Nurture new leads automatically.

Follow-up emails → Remind leads to book a call or complete a purchase.

Event reminders → Auto-send reminders for webinars or consults.

Best Tools:

- ActiveCampaign, ConvertKit, or Mailchimp.
- **FMA Marketing** (fully loaded, ready to go!).

2. Social Media Scheduling

Batch-create a month of content and schedule it.

Auto-recycle evergreen posts so your feed stays active.

Best Tools:

- Later, Hootsuite, Buffer, MeetEdgar.

- **FMA Marketing** (*includes* the content, 1 button to get the whole month scheduled!).

PRO TIP: Schedule posts **but** still do **one live session per week** for engagement.

3. Lead Capture & Funnel Workflows

Capture leads automatically with landing pages.

Tag & segment leads based on behavior (e.g., downloaded freebie but didn't book a call).

Follow-up automation → Trigger reminders based on actions.

Best Tools:

- ClickFunnels, Kartra, Zapier.
- **FMA Marketing** (seamless automation!).

4. Appointment Scheduling

Self-booking calendar for consultations.

Auto-reminders via email or SMS to reduce no-shows.

Best Tools:

- Acuity Scheduling, Calendly, JaneApp, Practice Better.
- **FMA Marketing** (HIPAA-compliant scheduling!).

5. Payment & Subscription Management

Auto-bill memberships & subscriptions.

Send payment reminders automatically.

Best Tools:

- Stripe, Square, Kajabi.
- **FMA Marketing** (built-in payment automation!).

Delegate These Tasks to a Virtual Assistant (VA)

Some tasks **still need a human touch.** That's where a **VA** (virtual assistant) comes in.

Social media engagement (replying to comments & DMs).

Lead follow-ups (personalized messages).

Blog posting & SEO optimization.

CRM updates & appointment confirmations.

PRO TIP: Use canned responses & templates so your VA stays on-brand.

The $25K Cry for Help, the VA Chaos, and Ignoring My Own Gut

Ah, marketing mistakes. I've made some doozies.

Like the time I spent **$25,000 a month** on a marketing agency because I was drowning and thought they'd swoop in and save me.

Spoiler: They did not.

Turns out, throwing money at your problems isn't a business strategy—it's just an expensive disappointment.

Or when I hired an *entire team of VAs*, each responsible for one tiny marketing task, thinking they'd magically assemble a marketing machine while I focused on, you know, **not micromanaging 14 people at once.** Shockingly, it didn't work. Turns out, people need *actual direction* to succeed. Who knew?

And my personal favorite: ignoring my own instincts because some "marketing expert" said their way was the *only* way. I *knew* the approach didn't align with my audience, but I did it anyway. Annnnd it flopped. Big time. Because if your marketing doesn't *feel* right to you, it won't resonate with your audience either.

So, if you're currently resisting the urge to hire a six-figure marketing savior, throwing spaghetti at the wall with no strategy, or ignoring your gut to follow someone else's "proven" system… **learn from my mistakes.**

Test your ideas before you invest big. Simplify before you scale. And for the love of all things holy, trust yourself. You know your audience better than any overpriced agency ever will.

ACTION STEPS: Fixing Your Marketing Leaks

Audit your marketing spend. Where are you wasting money?

Pick one automation tool to implement this week.

Set up a nurture sequence to follow up with leads automatically.

Choose ONE platform to focus on. Stop trying to be everywhere.

Track your results. If something isn't working, tweak it.

Next Up: Marketing in Healthcare & Weight Loss – Legal & Compliance

Now that we've cleaned up your marketing leaks, let's talk about something **practitioners often overlook—compliance.**

In Chapter 20, we'll chat about:

HIPAA, FTC, & FDA regulations—what you can and **can't** say.

How to market weight loss legally (without getting in trouble).

Action steps to ensure your marketing is **100% compliant.**

Because **a great marketing strategy won't help if you accidentally break the law.** Let's make sure you stay safe.

PS – full disclosure, I'm still pist about that $25k wasted. I wish I could tell you it was the only money wasted. Agghh.

It's a big part of why for our practitioners, we teach so many *different* ways to market. There is not just one way and it has to be **right** for that business owner and their audience.

No doubt it would cost me less to just teach one thing, but that's not how I roll and there is plenty of that out there already. I like being what one client said recently, a program that is **UNMATCHED** in the industry.

That feeds into my why – to provide accurate, ethical, and current information you can count on.

I also like making other mamas rich.

You can have more than one why!

Chapter 20 - Marketing in Healthcare & Weight Loss

How to Market Ethically, Stay Compliant, and Avoid Legal Nightmares

Not legal advice, friends - you need an attorney for that!

The Fine Line Between Great Marketing & a Legal Disaster

Marketing is about **attracting clients and building trust**, but if you're in **healthcare, weight loss, or functional medicine**, you have to **play by the rules**—or risk getting fined, shut down, or sued.

If you've ever wondered:

- Can I say this in my ad?
- Am I allowed to share patient results?
- How do I market weight loss without making false promises?

Then keep reading. We're touching on **HIPAA, FTC, and FDA** regulations—so you can market with **confidence** (and not end up in hot water).

Keep in mind we are sharing general smarts, but you need to be mindful of specific rules for your license and your state – that's where your attorney comes in.

HIPAA, FTC & FDA—What You Can and Can't Say

1. HIPAA (The Privacy Rule You Can't Ignore)

HIPAA (Health Insurance Portability and Accountability Act) protects **patient privacy**—and violations come with hefty fines.

What you **can't** do:

- Share patient testimonials without **written consent**
- Discuss patient cases **publicly**, even if you don't name them – you must hide all PHI.
- Post "before and after" photos without **signed release forms** (and some ad platforms don't like before/after photos)

What you **can** do:

- Share general case studies (no names, no identifiable details)
- Use **de-identified data** (e.g., "Over 80% of my patients see results in 12 weeks") – see FTC below for warnings on this.

- Get **written permission** for patient testimonials and success stories

PRO TIP: Always use **HIPAA-compliant email & storage tools** (like JaneApp, Practice Better, SimplePractice, or **FMA Marketing**).

2. FTC (Truth in Advertising Laws)

The **Federal Trade Commission (FTC)** regulates **false or misleading marketing claims**.

What you **can't** do:

- Promise **guaranteed results** ("Lose 10 lbs in 10 days—guaranteed!")
- Use **fake testimonials or stock photos** to misrepresent results
- Say your program is "clinically proven" if it's not backed by **real studies**

PRO TIP: Make sure any claims are typical or average claims and/or identify "not typical results" – check with FTC and legal advice for specific regulations.

What you **can** do:

- Use **disclaimers** (e.g., "Results may vary. These statements are based on individual cases.")
- Share **honest testimonials** with clear disclosures
- Say your program is "**science-backed**" if it's based on peer-reviewed research

PRO TIP: If you're unsure, **assume it's NOT allowed**—better safe than fined.

3. FDA (What You Can Say About Supplements & Treatments)

The **FDA (Food & Drug Administration)** regulates **health claims**—especially in weight loss, supplements, and functional medicine.

What you **can't** do:

- Claim a supplement **cures, prevents, or treats** disease
- As far as the FDA is concerned, only a Rx treats/cures a diagnosable disease.
- Say your product "**eliminates**" or "**reverses**" a condition
- Use **drug-like language** (e.g., "This supplement lowers blood pressure")

What you **can** do:

- Use **structure-function claims** (e.g., "Supports healthy digestion" instead of "Cures IBS")
- Say your approach is **"designed to support weight loss"** (not "burns fat")
- Reference **scientific studies** but don't claim direct **cause-and-effect**

PRO TIP: Add the disclaimer: *"These statements have not been evaluated by the FDA. This product/service is not intended to diagnose, treat, cure, or prevent any disease."*

NOTE: Don't let this discourage you from private practice, functional medicine, or holistic health – just know the rules and follow them. On a daily basis patients are having amazing results with their practitioners and coaches, there is a lot of room for big impact without stepping on the toes of traditional medicine.

How to Market Weight Loss Legally (Without Getting in Trouble)

Weight loss is **one of the most regulated** industries in marketing. Here's how to do it **ethically and avoid hot water**.

What to **avoid**:

- "Lose 30 lbs. fast—guaranteed!" → Guarantees are a gray-area best to avoid

- "This program works for everyone!" → False claims get flagged

- "This detox eliminates belly fat!" → Sounds like a **drug claim**

What to **use instead**:

- "Our program is designed to **support healthy weight loss**"

- "Most clients report feeling **more energized** and losing weight naturally"

- "This approach has been shown to **help regulate metabolism**"

NOTE: Want to see health claims that have been vetted by a bank of attorneys? Choose your favorite big-name practitioner-grade supplement company and look through their catalog.

PRO TIP: Some ad platforms have specific rules. For example, Facebook doesn't allow:

- Close-ups of **midriffs or overweight bellies** in weight loss ads

- Directly calling out a person's body in an ad (e.g., "Are you struggling with belly fat?") or using "you" especially in the first sentence.

The best approach? Talk about the feelings, challenges, and frustration dealing with weight and what's possible in life on the other side vs the exact pounds – that's what your potential patients are buying anyway.

Avoiding False Claims & Staying Safe

Here's how to **avoid the biggest potential legal mistakes** in marketing functional medicine. (Again, not an attorney, not legal advice!)

1. Don't Make Medical Claims

What to **avoid**:

- "This protocol reverses diabetes."

- "This supplement cures depression."

What to **say instead**:

- "This protocol is designed to **support balanced blood sugar**."

- "Many clients report feeling **more energized and emotionally balanced**."

The key difference? The second statement **suggests support**, while the first one **sounds like a medical cure** (which only FDA-approved drugs can claim).

2. Be Careful with Testimonials

Patient success stories are **powerful**, but they must be used **correctly**.

What to **avoid**:

- "Jane lost 50 lbs. on my program and you will too!"

What to **say instead**:

- "Jane lost 50 lbs. following our structured nutrition & movement plan. Results vary based on individual factors."

PRO TIP: Always include a disclaimer: *"Individual results may vary. Testimonials reflect personal experiences and are not a guarantee of results."*

3. Be Transparent About Pricing & Terms

FTC regulations require **honest, upfront pricing**.

What to **avoid**:

- Extra fees hidden in the fine print
- Subscription **cancellations** that are hard to find
- "Limited-time" discounts that **never expire** (fake urgency is illegal)

What to **do instead**:

- Be **clear about pricing & payment plans** – this doesn't mean you can't do no charge consults, it means don't have hidden additional fees.
- Make cancellation policies **easy to find**
- Use **authentic urgency** (e.g., "Spots are limited due to high demand.")

PRO TIP: If you use **payment plans**, clarify the **total cost upfront** to avoid complaints.

The Muumuu Mafia Rises: Why You Don't Need Permission to Take Up Space

Don't use "following the rules" as an excuse not to start because you are too afraid.

When I walked into that room full of internet bros, not a single one thought I belonged there. But guess what? Their opinions didn't matter. The numbers did.

And when I moved from the back of the room to the front, no one could ignore me anymore.

That's how this game works. No one is going to *give* you space. You take it. You build it. You own it.

People will underestimate you. Some will flat-out ignore you. Let them. Then go build something so undeniable, they have no choice but to notice.

Because *your* business, *your* voice, and *your* mission are bigger than their doubts.

So go build your damn empire. In a muumuu. Or whatever the heck you feel like wearing.

Maybe you're part of the bikini mafia? I can't relate, but I celebrate you. Go get 'em!

Action Steps: Making Sure Your Marketing is Compliant

Ready to **get legally safe** while marketing effectively? Here's what to do now & run all this by your attorney:

- **Check your website & ads.** Are you making any **medical claims**? Remove or revise them.

- **Review your patient testimonials.** Make sure you **have written consent** & proper disclaimers.

- **Update your weight loss messaging.** Avoid **guarantees** and **false promises**.

- **Ensure HIPAA compliance.** Use **secure platforms** for patient communications.

- **Add disclaimers where needed.** FDA & FTC regulations require transparency.

Next Up: Wrapping It All Up: Your Climb Higher Game Plan

You've made it through the **marketing minefield**, and now it's time to **bring it all together**.

In the Chapter 21, we'll:

- **Revisit The Climb Higher Board Game**—where you are now and where you want to go.
- **Break down your next steps**—because you don't have to master everything at once.
- **Set your 90-day marketing & business goals**—so you can keep climbing higher.

Marketing isn't about **doing everything at once**—it's about **building smart systems** that grow with you.

Let's finish strong.

PS – don't panic about "following the rules" or use it as an excuse to stop (or not start). It can feel overwhelming but it's just part of life and owning a business. Heck, even if you didn't own a business: legality, government, and taxes are just something we all face.

And there are **no guarantees in life**. You'll see some people cheat and get away with it – ignore them. Some people will do everything right and still have to deal with some hassles.

Remember you are building your **own** business and creating your own life. Go back to Chapter 7 with the 5 Money Myths. Just make more money. That will allow you to have big impact, serve more people, and handle any adversity that comes your way.

Hard to imagine that right now? That's okay. **You start where you start**. Just get into action and one foot in front of the other.

You've got this!

Chapter 21 - Wrapping It All Up - the Climb Higher Game

From Learning to Doing: Your Next Step Starts Now

Learning about marketing has been **intense, eye-opening, and maybe even a little overwhelming** at times. You've learned how to market smarter, nurture leads, sell effectively, and build a practice that isn't just profitable—but also sustainable.

But here's the most important thing: **None of this works unless you take action.**

This chapter is about **putting your knowledge into play** and making sure your next step isn't just another book to read — it's a move toward the practice and life you actually want.

Let's break it down

The Climb Higher Board Game—Where Are You Now?

If you remember from earlier in this book, we mapped out the **different stages of business growth**—from scrambling to get clients to running a **well-oiled, scalable practice**.

Take a moment and **assess where you are right now**:

Are you still in the "I just need patients!" phase? → Your focus should be on lead generation and a solid marketing system.

Are you getting clients but still feel stuck in a rollercoaster of income? → Time to refine your sales and offer structure.

Are you making money but drowning in the daily grind? →
You need automation, delegation, and smarter systems.

Are you ready to scale to the next level? → This is about
building your authority, expanding revenue streams, and
positioning yourself as a leader.

Knowing where you are helps **clarify your next move. No
one climbs the mountain in one giant leap.**

You start with one small, intentional step.

Start Where You Are (No One Masters It All at Once)

If this book has given you **a million ideas**, that's great—but
you don't need to implement all of them at once.

Let's break the cycle of:

- *Reading, feeling inspired, and then doing nothing.*
- *Trying to do everything at once, getting overwhelmed, and quitting.*

Instead, commit to this:

One step at a time.

One improvement at a time.

One shift at a time.

This is **a long game, not a sprint.**

You are building something incredible—but only if you keep moving forward.

Remember Your WHY—Your Mission Matters

Marketing, sales, systems, and revenue strategies are all important.

But the real reason you're here? **You want to help people.** (And you *know* WHY!)

There will be days when things feel hard—when tech glitches, marketing flops, and the pressure to do it all makes you wonder **why you're even bothering**.

On those days, come back to **why you started**.

You wanted to create a business where you could truly help people without burning out.

You wanted freedom—not just financially, but in your time, energy, and impact.

You wanted to change lives—without feeling trapped in a broken healthcare system.

That **mission matters**.

Your patients **need you to keep going**.

Your Next Best Step: Implementing TODAY

If you take nothing else from this book, take this: **Action creates clarity.**

Don't wait until you have the "perfect" strategy. **Start now. Adjust as you go.**

Choose one key takeaway from this book to act on <u>this week</u>. Maybe it's improving your marketing message, launching a webinar, or setting up your first nurture sequence.

Revisit your practice level & model—are you on the right track? If something feels **off**, don't ignore it. Adjust your strategy to align with your **ideal patient.**

Set a 90-day goal for your business growth. What do you want to accomplish in the next three months? **Make it specific, measurable, and actionable.**

Examples:

"I will enroll 10 new patients into my program."

"I will automate my lead generation so I don't have to chase clients."

"I will increase my revenue by 20% without adding more work hours."

Final Words: Keep Climbing Higher

You are not alone in this journey.

You are part of a movement.

You are creating a business **that doesn't just help patients— it builds a legacy**.

And that's not something that happens overnight.

No rush. No pressure. Just steady progress.

Keep taking one step forward.

Keep showing up.

Keep climbing higher.

The world needs what you have to offer. **Now go make it happen.**

Hugs,

Dr. Z

RESOURCES: Become a Practitioner

So, You've Read the Book...Now What?

First off, congratulations. You've made it through an entire book on marketing, sales, compliance, patient retention, and automating your practice. That alone puts you ahead of 99% of practitioners, health, and wellness professionals who are still winging it.

But before you ride off into the sunset with your newfound business wisdom, let's talk about what's next.

This Additional Resources section includes a wealth of information to help guide you in the next step in building (or scaling) your practice. Whether you're just getting started or fine-tuning your systems, **these tools, links, and insights will help you implement everything we've covered in a real, practical way.**

So, grab your coffee (or adaptogen-infused, sustainably sourced, non-toxic, all-natural beverage of choice), and let's dive in.

Functional Medicine Training Comparison Chart

Tired of opening 25 browser tabs, cross-referencing outdated PDFs, and playing email tag with different programs?

We did the heavy lifting for you.

p. 1 of 8

FUNCTIONAL MEDICINE TRAINING COMPARISON CHART

Program	Provider	Acronym	Target Audience	Cost	Duration	Clinical Training	Practice Building	Key Features
The Mentorship 3.0 (earn FMACP or FMACC)	The Dr. Z Functional Medicine Academy	FMA	Serves MD, DO, ND, DC, NP, PA, RN + in FMACP & nutritionists & health coaches in FMACC	Grab the handout to see the cost	90 days and then month-to-month as needed	☑ Clinical ☑ Lab Analysis ☑ Telemedicine ☑ Certification ☑ CE (cont. ed) ☑ Legal and compliance ☑ Live consults ☑ Lab Software	☑ Practice Launch ☑ Branding ☑ Marketing ☑ Sales ☑ Financial ☑ 1:1 Coaching ☑ Marketing Software ☑ Masterminds ☑ Find a Practitioner Search	FMA is the only fully comprehensive program known for 1:1 coaching and more live support than all other trainings. Gets new practices started or scaled faster than any other, while addressing both new/experienced practitioner legal, compliance, financial, marketing and sales challenges. Extensive clinical training & certification. Take the FMA Tour at https://TheDrZ.com or see Certifications HERE
FMCP-M or FMCP (coming 2026)	Institute for Functional Medicine	IFM	Only medical licenses and now separates by prescribing authority	Grab the handout to see the cost	4 years	☑ Clinical ☐ Lab Analysis ☐ Telemedicine ☑ Certification ☑ CE (cont. ed) ☐ Legal and compliance ☐ Live consults ☐ Lab Software	☐ Practice Launch ☐ Branding ☐ Marketing ☐ Sales ☐ Financial ☐ 1:1 Coaching ☐ Marketing Software ☐ Masterminds ☑ Find a Practitioner Search	IFM is one of the oldest Functional Medicine training programs. It was started by Susan and Jeffrey Bland, Ph.D. and currently operates under the leadership of CEO Amy R. Mack and the IFM board. IFM has certified approximately 2600 practitioners, runs an annual conference (in-person over the summer) and has partnered with a health coaching academy (FMCA). IFM is a non-profit organization and has a clinical focus & rigorous testing. Visit IFM HERE
Functional Medicine University (earn CFMP)	Functional Medicine University	FMU	Only medical licenses but not PhD	Grab the handout to see the cost	6-7 Months (10 hours/week)	☑ Clinical ☐ Lab Analysis ☐ Telemedicine ☑ Certification ☑ CE (cont. ed) ☐ Legal and compliance ☐ Live consults ☐ Lab Software	☐ Practice Launch ☐ Branding ☐ Marketing ☐ Sales ☐ Financial ☐ 1:1 Coaching ☐ Marketing Software ☐ Masterminds ☑ Find a Practitioner Search	FMU started in 2006 and main teacher is Ron Grisanti, D.C., DABCO, DACBN, MS, CFMP. Known for its completely online program and variety of CEs with affordable pricing. There were some mixed reviews about the dated information in some of the courses and guest lectures, but from the website it appears they do offer new webinars. You can check them out online HERE
American Academy of Anti-Aging Medicine (earn ABAARM)	American Academy of Anti-Aging Medicine	A4M	MD, DO only for ABAARM Board Certification. Other medical licenses for ABAAHP certification	Grab the handout to see the cost	1 - 2 years	☑ Clinical ☐ Lab Analysis ☑ Telemedicine ☑ Certification ☑ CE (cont. ed) ☐ Legal and compliance ☐ Live consults ☐ Lab Software	☐ Practice Launch ☐ Branding ☐ Marketing ☐ Sales ☐ Financial ☐ 1:1 Coaching ☐ Marketing Software ☐ Masterminds ☑ Find a Practitioner Search	A4M was founded in 1992 by Dr. Ronald Klatz and Dr. Robert Goldman. The Metabolic Medical Institute (MMI) serves as a branch of A4M and together A4M/MMI offer a range of stand-alone courses or even month long courses. Mostly caters to Family Medicine physicians (MD). There are also several conferences each year, a membership offering. Learn more about ABAARM Board Certification for MD/DO HERE and visit the A4M website HERE

The **Functional Medicine Training Comparison Chart** breaks down:

Cost (because nobody likes financial surprises).

Program duration (because time is money).

Clinical vs. business training (spoiler: some programs completely ignore the business side).

Who each program is best suited for (so you don't waste months on the wrong fit).

View the latest Functional Medicine Training Comparison Chart here:

PRO TIP: If you're in analysis-paralysis about training options, use the chart. It'll save you weeks of research.

How Do I Become a Functional Medicine Practitioner?

Introduction

If you're exploring a career in functional medicine or looking to expand your practice, you've likely realized how transformative this approach can be. Functional medicine doesn't just treat symptoms—it dives into the root causes of chronic and acute conditions, offering patients truly personalized care. For many practitioners, this shift is the answer to frustrations with conventional medicine's time constraints and *"one-size-fits-all"* solutions.

But knowing where to start can be daunting. Questions like *"Where do I find functional medicine training?"*, *"How do I become a functional medicine doctor?"*, and *"What's involved in starting a functional medicine practice?"* often come up. That's why we've created the **first and only comprehensive**

comparison chart of functional medicine training programs. This resource breaks down everything you need to know— **price, duration, features, and more**—so you can make an informed decision about your next steps.

You can dive into the chart right away or continue reading through the article:

Click **HERE** or type in **https://get.thedrz.com/FM-Chart-MMM**

Whether you're just beginning your journey or ready to start or grow your own practice, this article will guide you through the essentials of functional medicine training, help you understand the opportunities available, and provide actionable steps to help you achieve your goals. Let's dive in and discover the options that will help you transform your career and your patients' lives.

1. What is Functional Medicine?

Functional medicine is a **patient-centered approach** to healthcare that focuses on identifying and addressing the root causes of disease rather than simply managing symptoms. Unlike conventional medicine, which relies on standardized treatments for specific diagnoses due to a third-party payer system (health insurance) that necessitates bell-curve care and a predictive model based on "standard of care", functional medicine is built to handle the "outliers" at either end of the bell curve and a **personalized, customized, and individualized** approach for each person that walks through your clinic doors.

Practitioners work in partnership with their patients to focus on **"root-cause care"** and while the preference is for natural means whenever possible, functional medicine is **not** anti-medication or anti-surgery. It's important to not get stuck in any philosophical agenda, but to just give the best treatment possible to that individual patient. The best practitioners use and/or refer to the specialists and tools available to both conventional and functional medicine as needed.

At its core, functional medicine emphasizes the following principles:

- Treating the individual, not just the disease.
- Using evidence-based practices that integrate conventional and alternative therapies.
- Viewing the body as a whole, interconnected system rather than isolated organs.
- Empowering patients to take an active role in their health.

This approach is particularly **effective** for individuals dealing with chronic conditions, complex symptoms, or those seeking a preventative path to long-term health.

2. The History of Functional Medicine

Functional medicine has its roots in the mid-20th century when healthcare practitioners began exploring holistic and natural approaches to wellness. By the 1980s, doctors started utilizing advanced lab testing to identify imbalances in amino acids, fatty acids, vitamins, and other health markers, focusing on **personalized strategies** to address chronic health issues through nutrition, exercise, and supplementation.

The **term "Functional Medicine"** was officially introduced in 1990 by Jeffrey Bland, Ph.D., a biochemist and researcher known for his groundbreaking work in nutrition and health. He and his wife, Susan, went on to establish the first Functional Medicine Institute in 1991. Their seminars emphasized key areas such as gut health, immune function, hormone balance, and detoxification.

Since then, functional medicine has evolved from being viewed as an "alternative" practice to a *respected, integrative approach embraced by practitioners worldwide*. With growing patient demand for solutions to complex chronic conditions, functional medicine has gained recognition as a vital complement to conventional healthcare.

There are more schools and universities offering degrees in Functional Medicine and groundbreaking research and partnerships being formed such as the Cleveland Clinic Center for Functional Medicine.

While this is exciting and more to come, the vast majority of Functional Medicine practitioners already have some type of medical license, get certified through advanced training (check out our FM Training Comparison Chart), and operate their own private practice in person, hybrid, or via telemedicine.

3. Functional Medicine Practitioner Eligibility

Becoming a functional medicine practitioner typically requires a healthcare-related background. The eligibility requirements vary depending on the program, but most certifications and training options are designed for licensed medical professionals.

Eligible professionals typically include:

- Medical Doctors (MD)
- Doctors of Osteopathy (DO)
- Doctors of Chiropractic (DC)
- Naturopathic Doctors (ND)
- Dentists (DDS/DMD)
- Physician Assistants (PA)
- Nurse Practitioners (NP)
- Acupuncturists (LAc)
- Pharmacists (PharmD)
- Mental Health Professionals (e.g., Ph.D., Psy.D., LCSW)

Other healthcare providers eligible with specific degrees:

- Registered Nurses (RN)
- Registered Dietitians (RD)
- Occupational Therapists (OT)
- Physical Therapists (PT)

To qualify for certification programs like those offered by the Institute for Functional Medicine (IFM), or The Dr. Z Functional Medicine Academy (FMA), most applicants must have a bachelor's degree or higher in a health-related field.

However, some programs also have a certification for health coaching and nutritionists such as The Dr. Z Functional Medicine Academy's FMACC or Institute for Integrative Nutrition's (IIN) coaching certification. These programs offer exposure to the world of Functional Medicine that allows each professional to practice up to their individual scope of practice.

There is room for everyone in Functional Medicine, but it is very important to note that your medical license is what determines your scope. An MD will have access to all the tools in Functional Medicine along with the full breadth of what their license allows in conventional medicine. An NP can set up a private practice using Functional Medicine, but needs to be mindful of the specific license and state regulations which will determine if that NP can practice autonomously or needs a physician supervisor, same with PAs. A DC as a primary point of care chiropractic physician will be able to open a practice and operate independently, but must operate within their scope and won't have access to medications. A health coach can have a Functional Medicine focused practice that is of great service to their clients, but must be mindful to operate within their scope of education and won't diagnose or treat. This article is not designed to provide legal advice and your scope of practice varies state-to-state, please watch our legal training videos and utilize our referral list of attorneys for more information.

While your license or certification determines your "scope of practice", it does *not* determine your success in practice.

We have trained every level of practitioner from a triple-board certified physician to a health coach and every medical license in-between. How you set up your practice, your ability to be coachable and learn new entrepreneurial skills such as marketing will determine if you build a 6-figure, 7-figure, or even 8-figure practice.

4. Why Doctors, Nurses, PAs, & DCs Are Switching to Functional Medicine

Feeling **burnt out** in your current healthcare role? You're not alone. Studies consistently show that burnout rates among healthcare professionals—especially doctors, nurses, physician assistants (PAs), and chiropractors (DCs)—are alarmingly high. For physicians, nurses, and physician assistants, burnout rates are reported to be over 50%, and in some surveys, they climb as high as 80%. Long hours, high patient loads, and the relentless demands of an overburdened healthcare system leave little room for the meaningful, patient-centered work that most practitioners entered the field to provide. For chiropractors reporting burnout it stems from lower reimbursement rates with insurance, physical demands, high volume practice, and administrative isolation.

At its heart, **healthcare is about helping people heal**, but the current system often prioritizes quick fixes and volume over outcomes. Functional medicine offers an antidote. This approach allows practitioners to dig deeper, addressing the root causes of illness rather than merely treating symptoms. It empowers you to create lasting, transformative results for your patients while rekindling your passion for medicine.

Additionally, functional medicine fosters collaboration, offering a more supportive healthcare model. You're **no longer**

navigating complex cases alone—whether through shared knowledge, specialized tools, or a team-based approach, functional medicine provides the resources and environment to truly thrive in your practice. For many professionals, making the switch to functional medicine isn't just about a career change; it's about reclaiming the joy and purpose that brought them into healthcare in the first place.

5. How to Choose the Right Functional Medicine Training for You

Choosing the right functional medicine training program is more than just picking the best clinical curriculum—it's about finding a program that prepares you for both patient care *and* the business of running a practice. For many healthcare professionals, transitioning into functional medicine is also their first step into entrepreneurship. To succeed, you need training that not only deepens your clinical expertise but also equips you to build and manage a thriving practice.

Here are a few key factors to consider:

- **Comprehensive Clinical Education** Look for programs that provide a strong foundation in functional medicine principles, including root cause analysis, personalized treatment planning, and advanced lab interpretation. Ensure the curriculum aligns with your clinical interests and goals.

- **Business and Practice Management Skills** Starting and managing a functional medicine practice requires skills in marketing, patient acquisition, and operational efficiency. Prioritize training programs that include modules on building a practice, managing finances, and leveraging technology to streamline your workflow.

- **Flexible Formats** As a busy professional, you'll want a program that fits into your schedule. Many programs offer online or hybrid options, allowing you to learn at your own pace while balancing your current work commitments.

- **Support and Resources** Choose a program that offers ongoing support, such as mentorship, networking opportunities, and access to practice-building tools. Having a community of like-minded professionals can be invaluable as you grow your practice.

By selecting a program that addresses both clinical expertise and business acumen, you'll be better equipped to deliver transformative care for your patients while creating a sustainable and rewarding career in functional medicine

6. Training and Certifications in Functional Medicine

The Dr. Z Functional Medicine Academy (FMA)

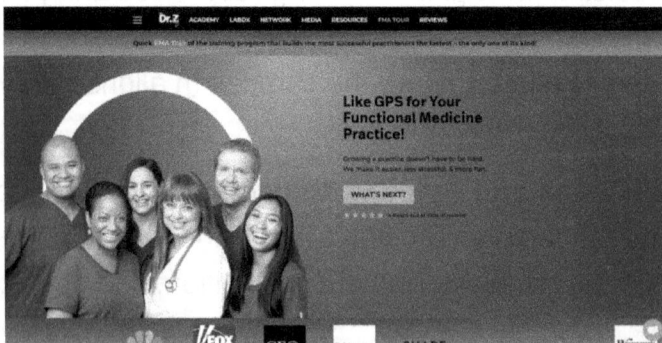

The Dr. Z Functional Medicine Academy (FMA) launched The Mentorship 3.0 last year which is **unprecedented** in Functional Medicine education - the only comprehensive clinical, practice building, and business growth training of its kind.

FMA was created in response to the lack of practical clinical training, absent marketing education, and confusion about ethical and responsible compliance laws observed by founder Dr. Z in existing functional medicine programs. While they all offered something of benefit, it was her mission to create one program that encompassed everything that was needed for the Functional Medicine practitioner with cutting-edge and contemporary information you could count on.

As a result, Dr. Z has personally invested over $500,000 in education, business training, HIPAA, legal, and financial compliance to make sure FMA is always ahead of the curve for the practitioners they serve.

The Mentorship 3.0 (earn FMACP or FMACC)

The Mentorship 3.0 (TM3.0) has evolved over the years to become your *"one-stop-shop"* for Functional Medicine practice success.

As a practitioner, the clinical training is unparalleled. You will earn your FMACP (Functional Medicine Academy Certified Practitioner) or FMACC (Certified Coach) depending on your current licensure. The training includes comprehensive online education for moving a patient through care, gastrointestinal health, cardiometabolic health, nutrition, weight loss, and functional endocrinology. A case review and certification test must be completed to be certified.

Additional clinical certifications are **included** in the program and may be completed at your pace in Pediatrics (the first comprehensive Functional Medicine Pediatrics certification), Advanced Hormones in Women, Mold Environmental Illness and Detoxification, and Lab Analysis. Upcoming certifications in 2025 include: Psychology, Dermatology, Advanced Hormones in Men, and Peptides. Certifications are included free of charge to current TM3.0 members.

Live Clinical Consults occur **daily** with the clinical staff and include topics such as functional nutrition, supplementation, lab analysis, reviewing patient intake forms, developing treatment protocols, adverse reactions and contraindications, or whatever questions you have clinically.

CE's are included for all types of nurses (NP, APRN, RN, etc.) and free of charge for the first part of 2025. CME's for MD, DO, PA, DC and other licenses are in progress.

Clinical tools are also included in the program such as LabDX which provides marker definition, therapeutic insight, lifestyle recommendations, and supplementation with dosage for over 60+ of the most popular advanced lab testing in Functional Medicine. The LabDX software is included free of charge to TM3.0 members or may be purchased separately. The intake forms, clinic policy, HIPAA compliance, and patient handouts for your EMR are also provided with substantial savings depending on which EMR you choose.

Practice setup, launch, and growth is part of what places FMA in a category of its own. Doctors and nurses who have never worked outside of the hospital routinely get FM certified, launch their practice, and sign their first new patients through FMA's unique "**Rx5 Formula**" for practice success. FMA practitioners celebrate their first $5-10k per month in new patient signups, then $20-50k per month, and you can watch this recent interview of an FMA client who just had her first $100k month - watch **HERE**.

There are many ways to market and grow your practice and FMA teaches them all - in exacting detail, plus offers more than 20 live classes each week to support you in everything from branding and design to social media and websites to basic marketing and advertising to no charge consults and sales.

FMA is unique in that it includes the FMA Marketing software free of charge to all TM3.0 members - which provides you with website templates, a toll-free phone number, email marketing, texting, social media scheduler and social media content (new each month), automated newsletters by niche, webinar funnels, quiz funnels, a full CRM, analytics and more, plus it is all HIPAA compliant. This marketing and sales software is included free of charge to TM3.0 members or may be purchased separately.

FMA recently launched **SearchFunctionalMedicine.com** (SFM) - the only "find-a-practitioner" search of its kind that showcases the multiple certification you may have earned, allows up to a 2,000 word bio, helps you get found with SEO-friendly links to your website and social media, and the only practitioner search engine that pulls in your Google Reviews as peer evidence is so helpful when the public is choosing a practitioner. They may also use advanced search by location, languages spoken, population served, and treatment specialty. Dr. Z has committed to using her vast knowledge and experience with Facebook advertising to run ads to the consumer public to help practitioners get found - essentially paying for ads for you in 2025. This listing is included free of charge to TM3.0 members or may be purchased separately.

When you are ready for staffing support, FMA has you covered. They have partnered to bring you VA Solutions which are reliable virtual assistant services to help with your tech and admin needs at a very affordable cost that may be purchased as needed, in small blocks, with no long term contracts.

Ready for support in fulfillment on the clinical side? No problem, no long contracts, no onboarding fees, no delays or having to spend months training new staff. FMA has partnered with the leading staffing agency for health coaches and clinical nutritionists. When you are ready, they have staff waiting for you to plug right into your new or existing clinical offerings. All services include a wealth of white-labeled clinical resources (nutrition guides, meal plans, menus and more) and unlimited patient-to-coach messaging all month long.

Legal, financial, and compliance are also at the heart of FMA and something we are uniquely positioned to speak on. While not an attorney or accountant, Dr. Z has worked with all the top Functional Medicine legal firms and can share information and provide valuable referrals (and sometimes discounts) as needed. Having such a varied exposure to every medical license, Dr. Z can present on the safest and most conservative measures to set up your practice so you can be in full compliance, protect your license, and rest easy while still having room to build an amazing practice and impact patient's lives. Her method which she calls "coloring within the legal lines" doesn't stop you from building a hugely successful practice, but does help protect you from the abundance of poor advice and downright illegal methods that show up in most online marketing and other Functional Medicine training. You'll want to watch FMA's legal training, tax/financial training, and utilize our referral list of attorneys, tax specialists, and accountants.

FMA is one of the few Functional Medicine training programs to include 1:1 coaching. You'll be assigned an MSA (Member Success Advisor) for individual, 2x monthly meetings and daily/weekly support in your Slack channel. You'll also have an SA (Strategic Advisor) who helps guide you through assessments (deep dive provided every 90 days and shorter assessment end of each month) to make sure you are on the right growth track - whether you are brand new to FM, in the early stages of your practice, or already well-established and ready to scale) and that you are clear on the next right steps needed to hit your goals. You'll always have two sets of eyes to assist you and monitor your progress - we track everything and take your success seriously.

You'll also have access to your peers in our exclusive TM3.0 Skool community where you'll find recordings of all our current clinical and business training. No one generates more contemporary and current content than FMA. Join Dr. Z live multiple times each month for cutting edge training that impacts Functional Medicine practitioners today. Recent training topics include: Immune Dysregulation and Depression, January Pre-Launch Planning, How to Run a Virtual Marketing Event, How to Create an Online Course, Bredesen/Recode Cliffs Notes & Supplementation Guide, HIPAA Compliance in FM, How to Create a Webinar Outline that Converts, Speak-to-Sell, How to Optimize a Facebook Group, Tax Season Prep, and Practitioner Tips for Using AI plus What to Avoid.

FMA Duration

90 days and then month to month. A high percentage of practitioners stay with FMA for years due to the unparalleled support and benefits - but that is up to you.

FMA Key Features

A fully comprehensive and "one stop shop" to Functional Medicine training. Whether this is your first FM program or going to be your last one, FMA will have something you need that is missing from the rest of what is currently available. You can read through an overview of FMA **HERE**.

FMA Notes

FMA describes its program as "practical and actionable for practitioners determined to succeed". If curious to learn more, talk to a Practice Advisor **https://link.thedrz.com/book-a-call-MMM**

By selecting a program that addresses both clinical expertise and business acumen, you'll be better equipped to deliver transformative care for your patients while creating a sustainable and rewarding career in functional medicine.

Closing

Functional Medicine is an exciting field and one that provides a unique opportunity where all levels - Business Owner, Practitioner, Staff, Patient/Client can benefit and feel good about the impact they are having in their lives and the world around them.

Choosing where to begin (or your next move) in your Functional Medicine training can feel daunting - we know our researchers spend hundreds of hours building the FM **Training Comparison Chart**!

As we sign off we'll share Top 10 Tips to choosing the right training with the hope that it will be helpful for you.

Top 10 Tips for Choosing Your Mentor aka 10 Criteria Before You Hire

- Do they understand Functional Medicine clinical **AND** business practices? Have they done it themselves?

- Do they understand how to market to potential patients **SPECIFIC** to Functional Medicine? Are they aware of FDA and FTC restrictions?

- Do they have **more than one method** or ability to modify/customize to meet your specific needs?

- Do they have a **blend** of "doing it yourself", "do it with you", and "done for you" services?

- What **accountability** and tracking is there in their program so you don't get lost or fall through the cracks?

- Do they have a **clear map** or method to move through their program and proven systems to get there?

- Have others **completed** their program and demonstrated success?

- What kind of **support** do they offer you? 1:1, group coaching, support calls? How often?

- Do **you like them** and want to learn from them? Do you trust them?

- Do they **INNOVATE** or are they stagnant? How **dated** is their material? Are they doing this right NOW in the same environment you are? Do they know what to do when things go wrong? What's plan B, C, & D? Are they IN it with you?

FM Training Chart Notes and Disclaimer

DEFINITIONS:

Program - the course, program, or class you would sign up for

Provider - The company that owns/operates that program

Target Audience - who the company markets to and/or the bulk of the students attending

Green checkmark - service was verified provided, level/capacity of service will still vary among providers

Yellow checkmark - service mentioned, appeared to be a smaller or incomplete aspect of the program

Red X-mark - service was not mentioned or not provided

DUE DILIGENCE:

Listing in the Functional Medicine Training Comparison Chart does **not** imply endorsement or validation of any kind. These are some of the online training companies that you will encounter upon performing a Google search and you must perform your own due diligence.

RESOURCES: Find a Practitioner

Finding the Right Practitioner for You

If you're ready to get to the root cause of your health challenges and experience truly personalized care, finding the right functional medicine practitioner is a crucial step. Functional medicine focuses on identifying and addressing the underlying causes of symptoms, rather than just managing them. Whether you're dealing with chronic issues, hormonal imbalances, digestive concerns, or simply want to optimize your health, a skilled practitioner can guide you toward lasting solutions tailored specifically to your needs.

When searching for a practitioner, consider your goals. Are you looking for someone local for in-person visits, or do you prefer the convenience of virtual care? Do you need someone who specializes in a particular area, such as hormone health, autoimmune conditions, or gut health? A functional medicine practitioner is trained to use advanced lab testing and personalized treatment strategies that integrate natural and conventional approaches, offering benefits like:

- **A whole-person approach** that considers your lifestyle, environment, and genetics.

- **Customized solutions** instead of one-size-fits-all treatments.

- **Proactive health strategies** to help you thrive, not just survive.

To make your search easier, visit **SearchFunctionalMedicine.com**. This no charge online tool allows you to search for practitioners by location, virtual or in-person availability, language preferences, certification, and specialties. With this resource, you can find a practitioner who fits your unique needs and start your journey toward better health – ask questions and do your due diligence.

Looking for a practitioner? Visit **HERE** at **https://SearchFunctionalMedicine.com**

RESOURCES: More Labs Less Time

Say Goodbye to Hours of Research Looking Up Every Abnormal Lab Marker

Love Functional Medicine Labs but Tired of How Much Time it Takes? Ready to Have The Answers at the Push of a Button?

If you've ever found yourself drowning in a sea of confusing lab results, we've got a life preserver for you. Meet The Dr. Z LabDx System —the future of lab analysis!

Are you tired of feeling overwhelmed by managing multiple labs, spending hours researching articles, and endlessly charting?

You're at the right place! It's time for you to consider the ONLY lab analysis tool that has all your favorite functional labs done for you!

Free training HERE: https://labdx.thedrz.com/software-training

2 Weeks Free Trial HERE: TheDrZLabDX.com

Learn More HERE: TheDrZ.com/LabDx

STREAMLINE LAB RESULTS:
Interpreting More in Less Time

LabDX: Transforming Lab Analysis

LabDX combines the trusted insights of your textbooks with powerful technology to streamline your workflow. Save hours of research time and deliver exceptional patient care, all from one easy-access platform.

SCAN THIS CODE TO GET STARTED

HERE'S WHY LABDX IS A MUST-HAVE FOR YOUR PRACTICE:

Comprehensive Lab Analysis: Seamlessly process GI MAPs, blood labs, DUTCH tests, OATS, SIBO breath tests, and more—all within a single system.

Live Expert Support: Gain access to a weekly live clinical lab class, where you can ask questions, review challenging cases, and get consultative guidance in real-time.

Streamlined Supplement Recommendations: Instantly view supplement options by ingredient, brand, and dosing, making patient care simple and effective - only available in the online LabDX software tool.

Efficiency Without Compromise: Generate a single, detailed PDF report for multiple labs and/or lab markers, saving hours of preparation without sacrificing quality or accuracy.

Always Up to Date: Stay ahead in your practice with new tests added monthly, ensuring access to the latest advancements in functional medicine.

LabDX takes the guesswork out of lab analysis and empowers you to deliver personalized care faster than ever. By combining cutting-edge technology with live weekly support, it's the ultimate tool for elevating your practice and achieving better outcomes for your patients.

Go **HERE** or type in **https://thedrz.com/labdx/** to see the LabDX demo or reach out via email at **team@thedrzlabdx.com**.

RESOURCES: Marketing Done For You

Automate Your Practice & Focus On What Matters Most…Your Patients

FMA Marketing – the all-in-one practice management system that handles your marketing, admin, and patient communication… while you focus on healing

You became a healer, not an administrative assistant

Is this your practice right now?

- Missed calls turning into missed opportunities
- Potential patients slipping through the crack

- Late-night hours spent on follow-up emails
- Manual scheduling eating up your team's time
- Patient messages scattered across different platform
- Important conversations getting lost or forgotten
- Weekend hours wasted on social media content
- Reviews and reputation management falling behind
- Staff overwhelmed by repetitive admin tasks
- New patient inquiries going unanswered for days

Sound familiar?

You're not alone. Most functional medicine practices lose up to 40% of potential patients simply due to poor communication systems and manual follow-up processes.

- Every missed call...
- Every delayed response...
- Every forgotten follow-up...

That's not just an administrative headache.

That's revenue walking out the door.

There's a better way.

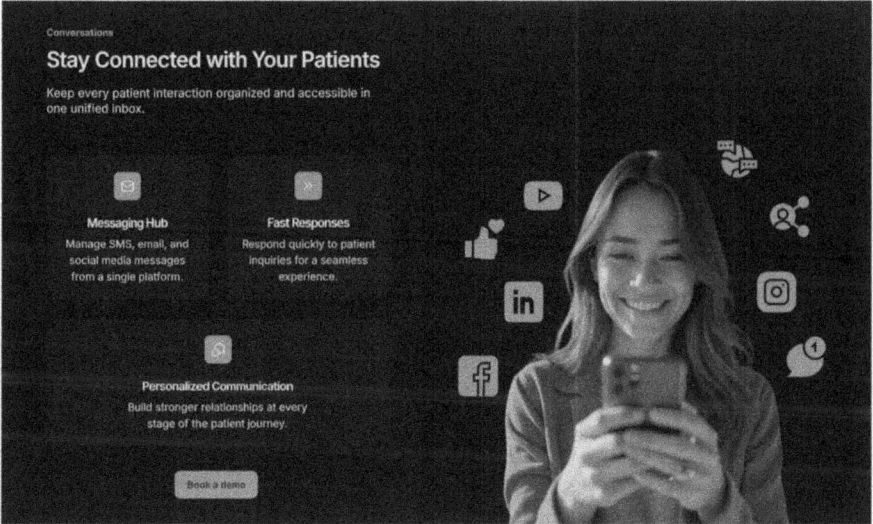

Your practice on autopilot –

Introducing FMA Marketing

One system to: Manage patients, Handle marketing, Ensure compliance, Scale your practice

Practice Management

- Unlimited scheduling
- Payment processing
- Patient CRM
- Mobile app access

Marketing Suite

- Website templates
- Email automation
- Social media management
- Content creation

Patient Communication

- SMS messaging
- Email campaigns
- Chat support
- Follow-up automation

Business Growth

- Sales funnels
- Lead magnets
- Course hosting
- Membership areas

Unleash The Full Power Of Data

Everything you need to convert, engage, and retain more users.

400+

Projects Completed

350+

Practitioners

100+

Hours Saved Weekly

BOOK A DEMO

★ ★ ★ ★ ★

FMA Marketing has been a literal gamechanger for my practice! I was wasting so much time and money before, its embarasssing!

— Joanne K

Functional Medicine Nurse Practitioner

★ ★ ★ ★ ★

My confidence in my business is way up. Social Media, Email Marketing done! Chat widget, ai answering my phone when I sleep...all the automations. Feels liberating!

— Dr. Nadia S

Functional Medicine Practitioner

Curious to learn more? Check out the details **HERE** or type in **https://thedrz.com/functional-medicine-automation/** and you can schedule a demo or just sign up.

Afterword

From Me, the Middle-Aged Mama in the Muumuu

I have taught for years that I believe business can be one of your **biggest teachers**. It asks so much of you and when you rise to the occasion, you feel like the heroic warrior that you are.

It doesn't mean you don't have those days where you feel defeated, hiding on the floor of the closet eating cookies – but that has to be temporary.

When you build your practice, it becomes your **baby**. You will pour into this business, be challenged by it, you will learn from it, and by creating something great you'll **be giving back to the world**.

In many ways, the more bumps you face, the stronger you will become.

So, while I wish you much ease and speed, I also want you to face the storms that teach you **that you are powerful**.

You have the ability to create a practice and life that you love.

But you must get into **action**.

Not just busy work, but action that produces results.

It's okay to be afraid, but do it anyway.

I have two favors to ask of you.

The first – if you found this book helpful at all, **I'd love if you would leave a review.** Not only does it help others find this book, but it makes my day. Sincerely, I thank you and my family thanks you. **Reviews are food for our soul**. You can leave them **HERE** or type in **https://thedrz.com/reviews/** and if you'd be willing to copy your review onto Amazon, I'd be over the moon!

The second – **come find me, because I'm waiting for you.**

I want to know what you thought of the book, what are you going to start doing, where are you in your practice, and how are things going? You can find me in our Facebook group **HERE** or type in **https://www.facebook.com/groups/functionalmedicineprac titioners**

Just tag me and say "Hi", I love talking to practitioners, health, and wellness coaches. Our work is important!

Most importantly – don't stop, don't quit – your greatest success is right around the corner.

Big hug,

Dr. Z

The Infamous Muumuu

Yeah, I wore it everywhere. "Hello Menopause, my old friend, I've come to talk with you again. Because a hot flash softly creeping, left its wetness while I was sleeping..."

bright orange, yellow, and blue – maybe the color will distract?

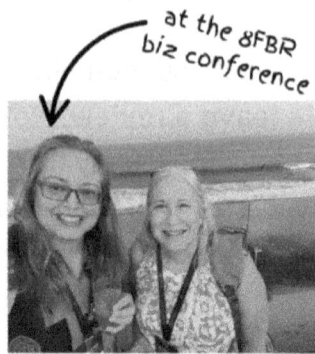

at the 8FBR biz conference

at my daughter's college graduation

with my entrepreneur mom

About the author

Dr. Brandy Zachary, DC, IFMCP, FMACP ("Dr. Z") was **never** supposed to be the one breaking marketing records.

She wasn't a bro in a sports car. She didn't have a trust fund or a secret stash of VC money. And she definitely wasn't rocking an **Instagram-worthy six-pack** while pointing at inspirational quotes.

But what she **did** have was a relentless drive, a deep love for Functional Medicine, and a refusal to accept that marketing had to be sleazy, soul-sucking, or only work for people named Chad.

So, she figured it out. **Took an offer from $0 to $7 million in under a year. Grew her business 150x. Won the highly coveted 2 Comma Club Award (only 1% of online businesses get this).** And she did it all wearing a muumuu.

Now, she's handing over her **no-BS, actually-fun-to-read playbook** to help practitioners, healers, coaches, and entrepreneurs **get clients, make money, and finally understand marketing in a way that doesn't make them want to scream into the void.**

Because if a **Middle-Aged Mama in a Muumuu** can build an empire, **so can you**.

Also by the author:

A Practitioner's Guide to Mastering Functional Medicine Lab Values - Foundations of Health Testing (Part 1 of 4) Base-Level Blood Labs, Cardiometabolic, and Nutritional Insights, published by Functional Medicine LabDX, Sheridan, WY 2025.

A Practitioner's Guide to Mastering Functional Medicine Lab Values - Gut & Digestion Insights: (Part 2 of 4) Advanced Testing for Gastrointestinal Health, published by Functional Medicine LabDX, Sheridan, WY 2025.

A Practitioner's Guide to Mastering Functional Medicine Lab Values - Hormonal Health & Balance: (Part 3 of 4) Panels for Reproductive, Adrenal, and Thyroid Function, published by Functional Medicine LabDX, Sheridan, WY 2025.

A Practitioner's Guide to Mastering Functional Medicine Lab Values - Metabolic Health & Toxin Testing: (Part 4 of 4) Autoimmunity, Toxins, and Advanced Metabolic Markers, published by Functional Medicine LabDX, Sheridan, WY 2025.

How to Read a Client From Across the Room: Win More Business with the Proven Character Code System, published by McGraw-Hill, NY 2012.

Looking for a practitioner? Want to be listed as a practitioner? Visit **www.SearchFunctionalMedicine.com**

Learn more about The Dr. Z Functional Medicine Academy (FMA): **HERE** or type in **https://thedrz.com/fma-tour/**

Chat about The Mentorship 3.0: **HERE** or type in **https://link.thedrz.com/book-a-call-MMM**

Curious about More Labs in Less Time? Check out LabDX **HERE** or type in **https://thedrz.com/labdx/**

Interested in FMA Marketing, the same software Dr. Z used to build a $1 million funnel? Visit **HERE** or type **https://thedrz.com/functional-medicine-automation/**